The FEAR of the BLOW

A YOUNG WOMAN'S GUT-WRENCHING STORY OF CHILD ABUSE,
DOMESTIC VIOLENCE, ALCOHOLISM, AND REDEMPTION

JENA PARKS

Copyright © 2017 Jena Parks

This Book is licensed for your personal enjoyment only. This Book may not be resold or given away to other people. If you would like to share this book with another person, please purchase an additional copy for each recipient. If you're reading this book and did not purchase it, or it was not purchased for your use only, then please return to Amazon.com and purchase your own copy. Thank you for respecting the hard work of this author.

Author's Disclaimer: To protect the innocent, some names and identifying details have been changed.

ISBN-13: 978-1542641401
ISBN-10: 1542641403

Preface

The abuse lasted for fifteen years. The journey to overcome it will last a lifetime.

It took a long time for me to stop asking God "Why?" I couldn't understand why the abuse was happening and why he didn't stop it. I must have asked him that same question thousands of times before realizing that the answer would be of no consequence. Looking back, I believe that God had great compassion for every single one of those desperate childhood pleas and that his inaction was guiding me to a more fruitful place.

I began to ask God "What?" *What do you want from me? What are you teaching me? What can I do to end this cycle of abuse?* I was at the very beginning of this new discovery, but I could tell there was real power in the answers to these questions. Power that could change my life.

I'd been waiting for so many years for someone to save me. And not just anyone. I wanted my dad to save me. Every young girl wants that. But I was going to have to accept the hard truth that my dad was a completely broken man who had long since given up on even being able to save himself. He couldn't save me. And the fight to save myself, my mom, and my brother had exhausted me in every possible way. It was like fighting to stay afloat in the ocean when each wave that hits you is stronger than the last. The effort is futile, but the will to survive is unrelenting.

I imagine that my dad started out just like me when he was a kid, fighting in every moment just to survive. But once free of his father's control and abuse, he continued fighting. It had become a significant part of who he was. He fought everyone over everything. It would take me many years and growing into adulthood to understand that my dad fought the hardest with those he loved and most feared losing. He played an inexhaustible game of defense to protect himself from the inevitable end. The one where love leads only to pain and suffering, betrayal and abuse.

I know well that convincing internal voice. My dad programmed me the same way his father programmed him, and we all lived out of that incredibly dysfunctional, fearful programming. No amount of intellect, logic, or rationale can reset those default switches.

I wasted more years than I care to admit chasing that elusive "reset" switch before finally coming to terms with the fact that I was going to have to accept that there was no way to undo all of the damage that had been done all those years ago. No. I was going to have to learn to love the woman staring back at me in the mirror and find a way to start living my life instead of merely surviving it. It meant I was going to have to stop trying to be who everyone else wanted me to be, who everyone else told me I could be and should be and just figure out for myself who I actually was. And then I had to figure out how to be the best me I could be. But in order to do that, I was going to have to stop running. Running from the fear of failure and of letting others down. Running from their expectations. In that way, I'd become just like my dad. He was a runner too. He ran by losing himself in the bottle every day so he didn't have to face his fears. My running was more literal. I ran from every person that ever tried to be close to me. I ran fast. I ran hard. I ran long. I ran until I was all alone. And when I arrived there, it felt good, like I was finally home. When we're lost and afraid, we tend to seek what's familiar. Being alone was normal to me; it was all I had ever known. And I'd come to believe that I was the only one in the world I could rely on.

I, too, was still fighting, even after my war had ended. But in every war there is a time to fight. And there is a time for surrender. And it isn't until the surrender comes that real change and healing can take place. Simple in theory. But so very hard to do. Especially when all you know is the fight.

What does it take to break this generational cycle of abuse? Everything. *It takes everything.* It takes what you don't have to give. It takes what you are most afraid to give. It isn't easy. It isn't pretty. It isn't fun. And it isn't without great failure. But it is fruitful. *It is worth it.*

My daily reminder: Surrender the fight. Trust. Forgive. Repeat.

Dedication

This book is dedicated, firstly, to my mom, the most beautiful and gentle soul I know. Your extraordinary grace and quiet strength have been a guiding light throughout my life, my anchor in every storm, and the calm in the aftermath. Your unconditional love and support are what allowed me to embark on this journey of healing and recovery. Having carried these shameful family secrets for so long, I'd come to believe the shame was mine. Through the writing of this book, I discovered that the only real way to diffuse the power of any secret is to shine a light on it. I'm grateful for this opportunity to finally lay them to rest.

And to my brother, whom I dearly love. No one could ever understand what it was like for us as kids, paralyzed by fear and desperate to escape the daily abuse of our alcoholic father, all while pretending to the outside world that everything was okay. While the cruelty we suffered at his hands is forever emblazoned in our hearts and minds, it didn't destroy us. We broke the cycle of alcoholism and abuse. That is a miracle in and of itself. I'm so proud of the man and father you've become. Please know that I did my best to safeguard your story while telling mine.

To my dad, whom I couldn't have imagined listing on my

dedication page when I began this process. I realize now that I have some important things I want to say to you. You harmed my mom, brother, and me so grievously for so many years. Repeating what you come from is never an excuse, but I understand that it is the reason. I didn't write this book to hurt you or to shame you. Though I want to be very clear on this—the shame is yours. It's all yours. I know that now, and so should you. I don't blame you for my adult missteps and mistakes because that would mean I'd also have to credit you with my triumphs and successes. I want you to know that I forgive you and that I've been praying for you for many years. Praying that God would heal your childhood wounds and ease your fears. I know how heavy that burden is, and I don't wish it upon anyone. I pray that you find a place of peace. It's not too late, until it is.

And, most importantly, I must dedicate this work to God, whom I met sitting in my closet at the age of eight, a trembling, petrified little girl unsure of how, or if, I would survive another day. You met me right where I was and changed my life through the most precious of gifts—faith. And though you didn't alter my circumstances for many years, from that point forward, I never felt like I was in it alone. You were always in the trenches with me. And you still are. When I felt your leading to write this book years ago, nothing I put down on paper seemed right and I didn't know why. Thank you for patiently bringing me to the place where I could surrender fully to you and allow myself to tell the whole story. Not just the sordid details about what happened to me as a child, but the real story that was happening in between the tragedies—the story of my relationship with you.

And to you, dear reader, thank you for coming on this very personal journey with me. I'm sharing the painful account of my childhood in such a public way so that others will know how real and pervasive domestic violence is. It doesn't discriminate; it affects people of every background, from all walks of life. And it has a generational stronghold on its victims that must be broken for the sake of future generations. Too many are still trapped inside a broken system that requires significant change to allow for their safe passage to a place of lasting stability and security. I'm so fortunate to still be here, to be able to tell my story. But there are countless non-survivors of domestic violence whose stories will never be told. I dedicate this book to everyone who has ever suffered in silence, been held hostage by fear and shame. We have to claim our voices and our stories to have any chance of ending the vicious cycle of abuse. And for everyone reading my story, please know with absolute certainty that no matter how heavy your burden or how great your suffering, there is hope. You just have to be willing to look up.

Jeremiah 29:11: "For I know the plans I have for you, plans to prosper you and not to harm you, plans to give you hope and a future."

Contents

Chapter 1 - Killing Me Slowly	1
Chapter 2 - Running for My Life	23
Chapter 3 - No Reprieve	51
Chapter 4 - The Picnic	67
Chapter 5 - I Won't Tell	85
Chapter 6 - A Close Watch	103
Chapter 7 - Someone Help Me!	113
Chapter 8 - Just Do It, Jena!	127
Chapter 9 - These Three	137
Chapter 10 - You Want Me to Do What?	147
Chapter 11 - You're Never Going to Live Like This Again!	159
Chapter 12 - The Last Race	177
About the Author	199

Chapter 1

Killing Me Slowly

With every cruel, degrading word my dad spoke to my mom; with every single punch to the face and kick to the body; every time he spat on her or threw his drink in her face, he was killing me slowly. He was destroying me from the inside out. He stole my innocence and took away all sense of safety and stability. He conditioned me to fear everything and to trust no one. Surviving him forced me to bury my heart and build my walls. Everything I would become, both intentionally and unintentionally, both good and bad, stemmed directly from the abuse I witnessed my mom suffer at the hands of my father for years. And being helpless to stop it was an unfathomable torment.

The very earliest memory of abuse I have is from when I was five years old. It was nighttime, and I was suffering through one of what would be many horrible ear infections. As I lay there in my bed crying, in so much pain, my mom came over to see what was wrong. She quickly assessed it was my ears again and picked me up and held me. As she rubbed my back, she told me she'd take me to the doctor first thing in the morning. We both knew that wasn't going to help me get through the night, but there was nothing that could be done. Even at that young age, I knew this kind of pain would require medicine in order for it to go away. It seemed like I was at the doctor's office every month for the same thing. It was excruciating, relentless pain, these recurring ear infections.

I was finally drifting back to sleep in my mother's arms, my cries subsiding, when my bedroom light suddenly flashed on and there was a loud noise. It startled my mom so much that she dropped me, though I quickly jumped to my feet, eyes still trying to adjust to the light. I heard my dad yell, "What in the hell is all the noise over here? You need to shut the hell up! I'm trying to sleep, dammit! Are you so stupid you can't even handle a crying kid? You're so fucking worthless. I don't know why the hell I married you!" I held onto my mom's leg and tried not to stare directly at my dad. I was scared to death. What was happening? I hadn't meant to wake him up. My ears just hurt so badly, I couldn't help but cry.

"Sorry, Richard, she can't help it, she has another ear infection, and she's in a lot of pain—"

My dad picked up the lamp on the stand by the door and threw it at us. It missed, but as it shattered to pieces against the wall behind us, he yelled, "I don't give a shit what the problem is, I want quiet in this damn house now! Do you think you can handle that, you dumb hillbilly?" He slammed the door closed, and a few seconds later, I heard his bedroom door slam shut.

My mom immediately knelt down to make sure I was okay, and I started to cry as she noticed the puddle I was standing in. I had wet myself, and I was so scared and embarrassed. I grabbed the pillow off my bed and pulled it to my face to muffle my cry and to hide my face from my mom.

She stroked my hair and said, "Jena, sweetie, it's okay. It's going to be okay. You're okay. Just stand there for a second while I grab some clean clothes for you, okay? And don't move, Jena, I don't want you to step in the glass."

Mom lifted me up out of the glass and took me over to the other side of my room and got me cleaned up. I still hadn't spoken a single word. I was concentrating so hard on trying not to cry out loud that I had begun to hyperventilate. My mom picked me up and walked back and forth across my room while talking gently to me until she calmed me.

"Jena, we're going to very quietly go downstairs and sleep on the couch, okay? Let's be as quiet as we can now."

She got a blanket from the hall closet and led me down the stairs. She gave me some Tylenol and then climbed behind me on the couch, and we lay down together, snuggled up as tightly as we could. My ears still hurt so badly, but the fear of my dad hurting us was greater, so I didn't cry again the rest of the night. I lay there in my mom's arms for what seemed like forever before fading off to sleep.

The next thing I knew, I heard my mom's voice, "Jena, honey, wake up. It's time to go to the doctor."

I felt so tired, like I had just fallen asleep a few minutes ago. As my eyes focused, I could see that Mom had been crying, and her face looked a little funny to me. I wasn't sure why. Like her cheek was puffy.

I got to my feet and just stood there looking at my mom. She tried to hurry me up the stairs but within a few seconds realized why I was hesitating, "No one's home but you and me, Jena. Your brother is at school and your dad left for work. It's okay."

I'm not sure why, but her saying that made the tears well up in my eyes, and they filled so full that I had a hard time seeing the stairs. Through the falling tears, I made my way into my room, which now looked good as new, minus the missing lamp. As I got dressed and brushed my teeth, I thought about what had happened the night before and tried to make sense of it as best a five-year-old could.

Why was my dad so mad at me? I didn't want to cry. I didn't want to be sick. Why didn't he care that I was hurting? Had he been trying to hurt us with the lamp? Why had he said such mean things to my mom? And what was a hillbilly? I didn't know the answers to any of these questions, but the heaviness of the whole thing was really hurting my heart. All morning I could barely keep the tears at bay. Even at the doctor's office, as much as my ears hurt, I thought only about what had happened at home and how scared I was. And sad. It hurt to think that my dad didn't care that I was in so much pain and that he was angry at me for crying. And as much as those things hurt me, it hurt even more thinking about the mean things he had said to my mom. What is a five-year-old to do with that? I mean, how do you put it in place and move past it? I didn't know. That incident birthed anxiety into my young life, and it would become my constant companion.

Whenever I would feel sick after that night, I would keep it to myself. No matter how much pain I was in or how bad I felt, I would not tell my mom or dad. This caused me so much additional pain and suffering through the years, as I would let things like strep throat get so bad that it would take weeks to cure. My mom would usually find out I was sick by noticing that I had a fever. Even then, if she asked me if I was feeling okay, I'd always assure her I felt fine.

I couldn't have known at the age of five that the abuse would become much more frequent and far worse in nature. It was a progression that, by the age of ten, I was sure would eventually culminate in death. I think it's hard for people who have never experienced domestic violence to understand how it can go on for so long, how it has the chance to escalate to such terrifying heights. But that's the thing about domestic violence—it's a silent killer. It lives in the darkness where its secrets grow roots. And everyone in its wake is ruled by fear, under the full control of their abuser and convinced the only way to survive it is to keep the secrets hidden away from the rest of the world—a world that wouldn't understand them or likely even believe them. In many cases of domestic violence, there's an unspoken but absolute understanding between abuser and victim: you get to live in exchange for your silence. The problem with that understanding is that when the abuser decides to revoke it, the victim usually doesn't see it coming.

One of my dad's favorite ways to strike fear into the three of us was to wrangle our bodies into positions where we couldn't breathe and felt like we were going to suffocate. He would lie on top of us or beside us and hold us in a chokehold with one arm while covering our noses and mouths with the other. And it was terrifying, every time. I can't count the times I thought I was going to die. I would fight with every ounce of strength in me to break free of his grasp, but it was futile. I was no match for his strength. He did this to my mom far more than to my brother, Nate, and me; and I remember standing over them many times, begging him to let her up. When he wouldn't, I'd jump on top of him and try with all my might to pry his hand off her nose and mouth. I was usually successful. He'd get up and laugh, like it was the funniest thing. I hated these sick games of his. They frightened me so much.

One day after school, when Nate and I got home, my mom told us to put our backpacks down and come into the living room. I was nine, and Nate was ten. I panicked, wondering what she was going to tell us, but I also remember thinking maybe it was good news—maybe my dad had died. That was such a hopeful moment, however brief it was.

"Come here, you two. We're going to play a game where we see who can hold their breath the longest, okay? It's a really good thing to be able to hold your breath for a long time. Especially because you both like to swim. Jena, do you want to go first?"

"Yes! I'll go first, Mom," I said as if I was about to do something that was so much fun. And for a brief second it was fun, until it dawned on me why we were really playing this game.

"Okay, Jena, I'm going to wrap my hand tightly over your mouth and nose so you can't breathe. Don't panic, it's just a game, so relax and start counting in your head. Whenever you feel like you've held your breath for as long as you can, just tap on my hand and we'll stop."

I counted to forty-one, which seemed good to me, though I'd

pushed myself to the point I felt faint. We played that game for what seemed like an hour or more. And when we were done, my mom told us we'd done a great job and that we'd keep practicing to get better and better.

Later, in my room, I lay on my bed thinking about how hard it must be on my mom, living in constant fear that my dad was going to kill Nate or me—so much so that she felt we needed to practice holding our breath. I know she felt helpless to defend us against this impossible-to-control monster. And it didn't help matters that he would tell her all the time that he'd kill Nate and me and bury us in the yard if she ever tried to leave him. She was paralyzed by the fear of that threat becoming a reality. And there wasn't one person living in our house that didn't believe he was fully capable of doing it.

As I rolled to my side and hugged my pillow, I thought about how powerless we were. My mom couldn't take us and leave or he'd kill us. And if we stayed, he might kill us. There weren't any good answers. Not only no easy way out, no way out period, not if we wanted to live. It was moments like these that I became so overwhelmed with the bleak reality of our lives that I had to get into motion, move, do whatever I could to stop thinking about it. So I jumped to my feet, changed my clothes, and headed outside to ride my bike. I played mental games with myself, like seeing how fast I could ride the same path through the field. I'd do it over and over, pushing myself to the point of exhaustion just so I could force a mental shutdown. The mind can only take so much. Fear can become an overwhelming burden.

One of the most devastating nights for me as a kid was when I was twelve, and my dad came home from work already pretty drunk. He was particularly angry that night when he walked through the door. Mom was putting dinner on the table, and he stormed through the kitchen and started berating her for anything and everything.

"What the hell is this? I don't want meatloaf! I'm so sick of the same shit you put on the table! This isn't fit for a pig!" He grabbed a handful of meatloaf out of the hot pan and smashed it into my mom's face.

In the blink of an eye, I was between them and begging him to stop. I tried to wrap up his arms with mine as if I was trying to hug him.

"Daddy, Daddy, please stop! Stop! Daddy! Please!" I cried over and over.

He tossed the meatloaf pan on the floor before heading down the hall toward the bedroom. I panicked, fearing that he was going to get one of his guns from the gun cabinet in their bedroom. As much as I wanted to stay in the kitchen and help Mom, I felt compelled to follow the biggest threat in the house. It was rare for him to come home already that drunk and angry. It would normally take him half the night to get there. And though I hated calling him "Daddy"—I didn't even like to refer to him as "Dad"—I'd learned that he liked it, and I was willing to do anything to help defuse the situation, no matter how degrading. Survival over dignity, every time. That was no contest for me.

"Daddy!" I yelled just as he was about to enter his room. He kept going. "Daddy! What's wrong?" I asked as I kept my eyes peeled on his every move. I glanced back and forth from the gun cabinet to him, gun cabinet to him. He went into his bathroom and slammed the door and locked it. I felt momentarily relieved as I sat down on the edge of their bed, contemplating my next move. My eyes couldn't help but focus on the huge gaping hole in the drywall right outside my parents' bathroom. That was the hole my mom's back had made when he'd picked her up and thrown her against it last week. My dad was usually quick to fix the damage that revealed his despicable behavior, but I guess since it was in their bedroom and no one except us ever went back there, he didn't feel a sense of urgency to repair it.

After a few more mind-racing minutes, I decided to quickly check the gun cabinet to see if it was locked. It almost never was; the key usually just dangled from the keyhole. It was unlocked, so I locked it and put the key in my pocket. Not that I thought he wouldn't break the glass to get to it if he really wanted to, but for the time being, it gave me a small sense of relief. At least I could warn everyone to get out of the house if he tried to open the cabinet. He had threatened to shoot my mom before, so I dreaded having these guns in their room. It worried me constantly.

It was because of all of his crazy threats that I had an intense need to monitor the "temperature" of things in our house at all times. I needed to know where everyone was, what the mood was, and how drunk my dad was so I could plan accordingly. My mind was never at rest. I was always figuring ways to keep us alive... and safe...but mostly alive, since I'd learned safe was too much to hope for.

I strained to hear what was going on in the bathroom but couldn't make out any noises, then I heard the toilet flush. The door opened, and my dad stepped out, facing me.

I could see tears in his eyes, which wasn't all that unusual, just maybe unusual in this setting. Typically, he would tear up when he talked about God or his dad or his brother who had died in a fire as a teenager. But I'd never seen him tear up after doing something mean to one of us.

"Jena, come on, let's go help your mom. Come on, let's go." He waved me off the bed.

I didn't know if he was tricking me, but I was willing to take the chance, so I just went with it, thinking I could build on this to salvage the rest of the night. I walked over to my dad and hugged him and told him it was going to be okay. There was no real meaning behind my show of comfort, but as I hugged him, he hugged me back and let out a deep cry, and all of a sudden my heart hurt for him too. I didn't want it to, but it did. I could feel his tears landing on the top of my head, and I wanted to cry too, but I didn't. After a few minutes, I took him by the hand. "Come on, Dad, let's go help Mom."

We headed down the hall hand in hand, and I led him into the kitchen where my brother was sitting at the table, looking down. My mom had already cleaned up the mess my dad had made. I could see a red mark on her face where the meatloaf had burned her.

"Mom, Dad and I wanted to see if we could help you."

My dad leaned over to my mom and buried his face in her hair and whispered, "I didn't mean to…"

Mom's eyes filled up, and I could tell she was having the same reaction that I had. My dad never ever said that he was sorry. Ever. And even though he didn't use those exact words, I could tell that he was. And I wanted to do everything I could to make sure everything stayed on this track, the safe track. I asked Dad to sit down at the table while I helped Mom get things ready. She warmed up some leftover chicken in place of the meatloaf, and we all sat down to eat together. No one spoke, but we were somehow comforted by my dad's show of remorse. After dinner, my dad went out to the garage like he often did, and my brother headed to the rec room to watch TV. I helped Mom clean up the dishes. I asked her if her face was okay, and she said that it was, but she would never tell me if it wasn't. When we were finished cleaning up the kitchen, we joined Nate in the TV room. I don't think Mom or I ever really tuned in to anything that was on the TV; we just used it as time to think. Nate, however, lost himself in his favorite shows. It was his way of escaping our desperate circumstances. We each had our own unique way of coping with the hell we were living.

After an hour or so, my dad came back through the door, and he seemed substantially drunker than he had been when he had gotten home. I could tell by the way he fumbled to open the door. My heart sank and my stomach knotted up. The whole room got tense.

"What's for des...sssert?" he slurred.

"We have ice cream," my Mom offered.

"I don't want iceeee crrreeam! I bust my ass at work to provide a good living, and all you have for dessssert is iceee cream!"

He lunged toward Mom from the back of the couch, smacked

the side of her face, and grabbed her hair. "You better get your ass in that kitchen and find me something better than ice cream!"

My mom ducked out of his grasp and jumped to her feet.

"Dad! I'll make you something! What do you want? Dad, what do you want for dessert?" I asked, trying to distract his attention away from my mom.

But he was looking past me with those crazed eyes of his, fixated on my mom. I could tell he wanted to fight.

"Daddy, I'll make you some dessert! Come on, let's go in the kitchen!" I tried to take hold of his hand while keeping my head back at a greater distance than usual. I leaned away from him but reached for his hand. He swatted me away.

"I want your mother to get her ass in the kitchen and make me something! I'm the king of this house! And I damn sight better be treated like it!"

My mom had already moved quickly around the side of the couch and into the kitchen. I stayed strategically positioned in between as an obstacle, but he stumbled past me into the kitchen and lunged at my mom. He hit her in the face before I could get in front of him.

"You fucking worthless bitch! Who the hell would want you? Look at you! You're ugly, you can't cook—you can't do anything right!" He lunged for her again, but I was able to push him back hard enough that his blow didn't reach her. As my mom darted down the hall toward the bedroom, I thought, *No, Mom, anywhere but the bedroom! The guns are in the bedroom!*

He made a beeline for the bedroom but wasn't steady enough

on his feet to beat me there. I was terrified that he would have us cornered in the room with the guns with no way out except through him.

He pounced on my mom and knocked her to the ground.

"That's where you belong, you pig! On the ground! Now squeal like a little piggy! Come on! Oink! Oink! Let me hear it!"

As my mom tried to shield herself on the floor, I wrapped my whole body around his legs and squeezed with all my might so he couldn't move, but he'd already grabbed hold of my mom's nose and was pinching it as tightly as he could. I was afraid he was going to pull it right off of her face.

"Daddy, stop! Let her go please! You're hurting her!"

"Now squeal like a little pig! Let me hear it! I'm not letting go until you squeal like the pig you are! Oink! Oink! Let me hear it, dammit!"

He broke free one of his legs and was right on top of my mom with me still sandwiched in the middle.

"I said squeal like a pig! I'll pull your fucking nose off! Now squeal!"

"Oink! Oink! Oink!" I yelled. "Oink! Oink!"

I didn't know if he thought it was my mom saying it or if me saying it startled him, but he let go.

"Now stay down there! Don't you dare get up! Walking is for people, and you're just a little pig!"

With that, he left the room, and I wrapped myself around my Mom and just cried and cried. My mom cried too but she didn't say anything. She rarely said anything after an attack. I would try to comfort her as best I could, but let's face it, there was no real comfort to be had. Surviving was the best we could hope for.

There was always the moment right after the attack when we weren't sure if it was actually over yet or if it was going to continue. I never got any better at deciphering that. You just had to wait and see.

After several minutes, my mom got to her feet, and I followed suit. We just stood there, unsure of what to do. You're always so grateful for a break in the battle that you don't want to do anything that causes it to start up again. All too soon, we heard his footsteps coming down the hall, and we braced ourselves.

He barreled through the door with a drink in his hand. "Did I tell you that you could get up, little pig?" he screamed as he hurled his drink in her face, ice and all. As the whiskey dripped down my mom's face, he continued his verbal tirade, "You can't even listen, you're so stupid! You're just a stupid little pig!"

I began to beg, "Dad, stop! Just stop! Please! Go away! Just stop! Look what you did! Stop! Please! Dad!"

He never responded to me during these brutal attacks on my mom. I never knew if he pretended I wasn't there or he just didn't care that I was seeing and hearing everything. But he never acknowledged me, never let me know that he heard my pleas. But I still felt like my begging and pleading and getting in his way diverted some of the harm away from my mom. I had to believe that. I needed to believe that.

He turned to leave for what I prayed was the last time, and I grabbed a towel from their bathroom for my mom. She wiped the whiskey off of her face, hugged me, and said she needed to jump in the shower. I let go of her, but my mind started to race because I didn't think getting in the shower right now was the best idea. We didn't even know if it was over. What if he came after her again and she was trapped in the shower? I couldn't stand the thought of that, so I waited until she got in, opened the bathroom door, pushed in the lock, and shut the door. Locking doors in our house infuriated my dad, but I needed some time to figure out what to do if he came back for her. I couldn't just leave her so vulnerable in such a confined space. I sat on the bed while she showered and prayed the whole time.

God, please help us! I know you saw what my dad just did. And I know that you know we are helpless to stop him. I try. I really try! But he's stronger than me! But, God, he's not stronger than you. Why won't you help us? I don't even have any words left. I don't know how else to ask you for help. My mom is so little. She's barely five feet tall, God. What is she supposed to do? Please just let it be over for tonight. Please let him pass out so we can sleep. I know you're not going to kill him because I've asked you to do that a million times and he's still here. Still hurting us so badly. Why do I talk to you so much? Why are you the only one I ever tell all of this to? You never make him stop. Am I doing something wrong, God? I only pray for you to kill my dad because he's going to kill one of us if you don't. I just want it to stop, God. I can't take watching my dad hurt my mom anymore. I can't take it. It's killing me.

The bathroom door opened, and I was stirred out of my deep conversation with God. I searched my mom's face to see how she was, but she never gave anything away. She was somehow able to remain calm in the face of the worst possible storm. I, however, was very vocal, begging and pleading all the time. I'd say or do anything that I thought might head it off or make it stop.

As Mom headed to her closet to get dressed, I headed back out through the house to see where Nate was. The door to his room was closed, so I touched the handle to see if it was locked, and it was. That was a relief. Okay, now to see where Dad was. I passed through the sitting room bordering the kitchen, and as I entered the kitchen, my dad jumped out from behind the wall and scared me. I about jumped out of my skin. He did this kind of crap all the time. He thought it was funny, but I never did. My dad had a very twisted sense of humor. Thankfully, he passed out on the couch in the rec room a half hour later, and my mom and I were able to get some sleep.

His cruelty and twisted sense of humor were never more evident than one night at home when I was only eight years old. We were all watching the news on TV after dinner, and there was a story about a little girl who had been kidnapped. I found it so scary, and I climbed up on the couch next to my mom as the man on the news described how it all had happened. Afterward, I kept asking my mom whether she thought the girl was okay and if she would be able to go back home to her mom and dad. My dad spoke up, "Nah, she's dead by now. He snuck her out of her bedroom window in the middle of the night and killed her. Her parents will never see her again."

I started crying. I was petrified.

"You know, Jena, he's probably going to be outside your bedroom window tonight."

"Richard! That's enough!" my mom yelled. And my mom never yelled, about anything. "Tell her you're just kidding!"

He was unmoved by her plea, of course.

"Honey, your dad is kidding. He didn't mean it. No one is going to hurt you, and no one is outside your bedroom window! I promise. Okay?"

But the damage was done and the seed already planted. I just knew that bad man was going to get me next.

"I don't know, Jena, I think he likes to take bad little girls that backtalk their fathers all the time," he said with a grin.

I just buried my face in my mom's shoulder and tried to hide my tears. A half hour later, when it was time for bed, I announced that I would be sleeping with them.

"Sure, hon—" my mom started to say before my dad interrupted her.

"No, Jena, you'll be sleeping in your own room tonight," he said, smiling.

There was no way I was sleeping in my own room all by myself! I'd sleep on the floor in Nate's room if I had to, even though he hated it when I did that.

My dad headed to the kitchen, and I pleaded with Mom to let me sleep in her room. I felt like I was begging for my very life. One of my two bedroom windows was right beside my bed. There was no way I could sleep in there now!

"Jena, why don't you go get your pajamas on and then come over to our room?"

"Don't let him lock me out, Mom! Okay? Don't let him!"

"I won't, Jena. It's going to be okay. Go get your pajamas on."

I didn't feel confident that she was going to be able to get me in her room, but I headed down the hall to my room to get changed anyway. I peeked around every corner checking for the bad man. Once in my room, I immediately looked under my bed and checked to make sure the two windows were locked. They were. As I walked over to my dresser to get my PJs, I heard a noise and froze. My heart started pounding.

"AAAAAAAAHHHHHHHHHHHHHHHHHHH!!!!!" my Dad yelled as he jumped out of my closet.

I was so frightened that I wet myself, and then I fell to my knees and started crying.

"Oh, you're fine! Don't be such a big baby!" He walked out of my room laughing.

I sat there unable to move. My mom came running down the hall when she heard my dad yelling, and when she saw me there on the floor she was frantic. "Jena, what happened? Tell me!"

When I told her what had happened, she kneeled down beside me and wrapped her arms around me. That was when she noticed that the carpet was wet.

"Aww, Jena, come here, stand up, sweetie. Don't worry, I'm here, it's okay. You're okay. Let's go the bathroom and get you cleaned up."

She ran a warm bath and told me I could sleep in their room. It was still hard for me to speak without crying, but I told her I didn't want to sleep in their room because my dad was going to scare me again. She promised that he wouldn't, but I didn't trust him, so she told Nate to let me sleep on the floor in his room. Once Mom had said goodnight and left, Nate told me to get out. I pleaded with him to let me stay, but he said no. As scared as I was, I had to go sleep in my own room.

As soon as I walked through the door and saw the windows, I was petrified. I rechecked all the possible hiding places in my room to make sure no one was in there and made sure the windows were still locked, then I crawled into my bed and positioned myself on the side furthest away from the window. I lay there forever, unable to sleep. I don't even know how to adequately describe the intensity of the fear that gripped me. I was sure that the bad man was outside my window. Fear overtook me and I started to cry.

God, please, please help me! I'm so scared! And I'm all by myself. I don't want that bad man to take me. Please! I'm really scared, God. Really, really scared. Please keep me safe.

I couldn't shake the fear. Sweat beads formed on my brow, and I thought I was going to throw up. Finally, I grabbed my pillow and comforter off my bed and climbed into my closet and closed the doors. I thought maybe the bad man wouldn't be able to find me in there. Once I got all snug inside my closet, I just kept talking to God.

I didn't really know that much about God yet, but I knew that I believed in him. I was sure about that. And I was learning all about him in Sunday school. My dad's sister, Aunt Renee, talked about him all the time. Talking to him just made me feel better. But as I sat there in my closet, I was still so afraid. I started to cry so hard that I had to put my face in the pillow so I didn't wake up my dad.

Then the strangest thing happened. I heard a voice say, *"Jena, you're safe. I'm right here with you."* It wasn't an audible voice that you would hear out loud, but those exact words just filtered through my head, plain as day. Someone said them to me! I wasn't sure what had just happened, but I knew what I had heard. I sat very still, thinking maybe I'd hear it again. I strained to listen. Nothing. But I felt a warmth and calmness flood over me. It was indescribable. I'd never felt anything like it before. I knew with absolute certainty that it was God. He was there with me, and he was talking to me! I heard him so plainly in my head. And my fear…it was gone! All the way gone. I felt frozen in place, but not because I was scared. I was no longer scared at all. My mind was racing but not from the usual feelings of terror.

"God?" I whispered. *"Is that you?"*

I waited for several minutes, sitting as still as I could, but I didn't hear anything more. I so badly wanted to hear him again. To talk to God. I couldn't believe how I felt. I wasn't scared at all, and I felt lighter somehow, like I was no longer carrying the weight of the world around with me. After a few more minutes, I climbed out of my closet, got back in bed, and drifted off to sleep.

When I awoke the next morning, I was so excited. I didn't even know what to do with myself. I wanted to tell everyone that I had met God last night, but as the thought went through my head, I realized how it sounded. Everyone would think I had lost my mind. But it was true! And I knew it. I mean, I knew it. I had no doubt that God had rescued me last night. I had felt him there with me. And I had heard him! And he'd taken away all of my fear in an instant! How else could that have happened when I had never been so afraid in my entire life? I bounced out of bed and down the hall and found my mom in the kitchen cooking breakfast.

"Hi, Mom!" I said, far more chipper than would ever be expected from me in the morning.

"Well, hi, Jena. How are you this morning?" she said, smiling back at me.

I was bursting at the seams to tell her what happened to me last night. "I'm good, Mom. Can I tell you something?" I just couldn't contain myself any longer.

"Sure, what?"

"You have to believe me, okay? Because it really happened. It really, really did…I met God last night! He talked to me!"

"Well, that's wonderful, Jena!" my mom said as she fought back the tears.

"Mom, are you crying? Why are you crying?" I was puzzled that what I had just told her would make her cry. It wasn't sad at all. This was the best thing that had ever happened to me. A miraculous thing!

"I'm happy for you, Jena, that's all. They are happy tears."

I wondered what in the world happy tears were, but before I could ask, my mom explained that I was too young to know what happy tears were yet.

"Mom, has God ever talked to you before?" I had to know.

"Sure he has. Many times."

I was so relieved to hear her say that because it meant she wouldn't think that I was crazy.

"Isn't it so great, Mom?"

"Yes, honey, it is." She brushed my hair back out of my face and kissed my cheek.

I'll never forget meeting God that night, sitting in my closet. Never. As long as I live. I climbed in my bedroom closet that night a terrorized little girl, and I walked out with the greatest gift a person could ever hope to receive—faith. Absolute faith that God really does exist and he's exactly who he says he is.

Meeting God that night didn't change my circumstances, not by a long shot, and not for a long time. But it changed me, and it gave all my future conversations with God a much deeper meaning. I finally knew who I was talking to, and I trusted in who I was talking to. And that's why I never wavered in my belief that God was real. I couldn't explain his inaction, and I still didn't understand him, but I had no doubt that he was real. And that was good enough for me.

Chapter 2

Running for My Life

I can't pinpoint exactly when it was that I became the keeper of the secrets of the redwood house on Grant Road. But as I leaned up against the rough brick exterior of my high school on a muggy afternoon in May, I couldn't help but wonder if my life would be different if I had found the courage to tell someone what was happening inside those four walls. No one had any idea of the atrocities taking place inside that house. My house. The one I grew up in. The one I disappeared in.

Fifteen going on thirty, it seemed, I sat there contemplating every moment that had led up to this one. I hardly noticed how the freshly cut grass was irritating my bare legs. Just moments before on the track, I'd made a declaration I wasn't allowed to make.

"I'm so sick of this! I quit!" The words had exploded out of my mouth to my track coach with my shocked teammates looking on. I didn't give him or anyone else a chance to respond, I just stormed off the track and ran into the locker room, slamming every door and locker I could get my hands on as I passed by. I grabbed my clothes and shoes, shoved them in my bag, and headed for the door. My feeling of liberation quickly turned to intense fear, and I had a sinking feeling in the pit of my stomach.

To my classmates looking in from the outside, it looked like I had it made. I was Jena Parks, one of the most popular girls in the school. I was a tall, pretty, slender brunette with long flowing hair and big almond-shaped eyes, a decorated athlete, an honor roll student, a member of homecoming court, and prom queen. Sounds great, I know. What more could a teenage girl hope for? But the girl they thought had it made was a figment of their imaginations. She didn't exist. Her world, her reality was altogether different. Her life was far darker than anyone could have imagined. But perception is a powerful thing and dangerous when mistaken for truth. It's shocking how wrong we can get things.

Earlier that same day, as I sat in my homeroom class—there, but not really there, never really there—I heard the girl reading the morning announcements say, "…and congratulations to the girls' track team for their win last night over Massena Park. Placing first in the high jump, Jena Parks; first in the long jump, Jena Parks; first in the triple jump, Jena Parks; first in the 100 meters, Jena Parks; first in the 200 meters, Jena Parks; first in the 400 meters, Jena Parks…" As my classmates congratulated and teased me, I forced a smile, but I was sick to my stomach, reeling on the inside. Nervous. Anxious. And full of dread. I hated track. With a passion. Even hearing it being talked about on the morning announcements was enough to send me into a panic. I never chose to participate in it. It was not optional for me. It was a sport my dad had chosen for me. I was going to run. I was going to win. Every time. All the time. Period. The pressure my dad put on me as a kid was enormous. The pressure to win. To be the best. And not at anything important really, not at anything that actually mattered.

How telling then, my coach's preseason interview in the local newspaper summing up our team. "One of the fastest people in the school is Jena Parks. She ran a 57-second quarter mile goofing around in gym class—unbelievable. Parks is very talented but she gets real tight under pressure. Her potential in sprints is almost unlimited. She does long jump and triple jump. She can do anything 400 meters down. I'd be willing to bet she can beat anybody in the school, including most of the boys. Folding under pressure is the only thing that I can see stopping her."

When I saw that article in the newspaper, I was furious. Even though I was new to this team, I had been running track for this same coach under extreme duress since middle school, and he'd never once tried to figure out what was going on with me. He'd never asked me why I felt so much pressure or why I threw up before every single race. I don't think he cared about any of that. He simply reveled in the fact that he had the best female sprinter in the entire district in his arsenal. I hadn't lost a single district race since the sixth grade. By this time, I had come to believe that God had orchestrated all of the winning because he knew the penalty I faced at home if I lost. I just thought it was God's way of extending mercy to a very desperate, scared kid. Maybe that sounds strange, but that's what I believed. It was the only thing that made any sense to me.

As I sat through the rest of homeroom and morning announcements, I thought about how agonizing track season was and how none of my new teammates even wanted me on the team. The seemed to hate my guts, which made an already high-anxiety existence even worse. I dreaded being on this team for so many reasons. There were two juniors on the team, Laura and Jessica, who were known throughout the school for being top sprinters in the district. They had won almost every track and field honor with the exception of a state title. And then there was Cara, a girl who had proclaimed us mortal enemies, though I'd never even had one direct conversation with her. It seemed so ridiculous to me that a girl I didn't even know did so much trash-talking about me around school. But then again, I thought almost everything about high school was ridiculous.

Cara was also very popular, an extremely talented athlete, and I heard through the grapevine before the season even started that she was eager to race me. Just a few weeks earlier, the first day of varsity track practice had seemed more like a circus than a practice. Many students had been talking earlier in the day about a faceoff that was going to take place—Cara against me in the 400, her coveted race and my best event. I had no interest in participating in this contest, and I had done nothing to encourage it or egg it on. As the school day ended and the halls filled with kids either racing for the front doors or for practice, I made my way into the locker room at a turtle's pace. I waited long enough that everyone else was already out on the track before I even changed my clothes. I didn't want to see or deal with anyone on my team before the start of practice.

I pushed open the black metal door leading out to the field and saw an enormous crowd of people gathered around the starting line of the 400. Coach White had bought into the hype of this whole imagined rivalry between Cara and me, and the second I made my way to where everyone else was gathered, he said, "Okay, Parks, on the line." Not, how is everyone doing this year? Is everyone looking forward to a winning season? Let's begin by stretching. Uh-uh. None of that.

"On the line for what?" I said, unable to hide my annoyance.

"You know what, Parks. Let's get this race out of the way so we can all get on with practice."

Cara was smirking at me and whispering to a group of girls on the team. I knew they were willing a crippling defeat on me. I wanted so badly to just disappear.

We lined up, and Coach White blew the whistle and we were off! I took off like a scared deer that's just heard a gunshot. My mind was racing but not with any discernable thoughts. By the time I hit the first corner, I could no longer hear Cara's footsteps behind me, but I kept running like my life depended on it. I'm not sure I even took a breath all the way around the track, but less than a minute later, I crossed the line with time to turn around and watch Cara cross seconds behind me. I was so winded I could hardly catch my breath. Coach White patted me on the back and said, "Nice job, JP, now get those hands above your head and walk it off. You need to get some air back in those lungs! You gotta remember to breathe when you run, Jena. You look like you're holding your breath. You're going to pass out one of these days if you keep doing that!"

Though Cara was undoubtedly the coach's pet, I am certain he'd known how this race was going to turn out before we ever took the starting line. And, strangely, he was happy about the way it turned out. Like it gave credence to his preseason prediction that I could beat anyone in the school. I was certainly not his favorite student athlete by any measure, but I was his prized sprinter, and when I won, it was a personal credit to him. He was like my dad in that sense. My winning elevated him, and they both thought it was a reflection on them somehow. I never quite understood that. It's not like either of them taught me how to run. You either have speed or you don't. Regardless, I was just so relieved the race was over.

But it was perhaps the quietest win ever. I never said anything after a win, never celebrated a single victory, never smiled after, never raised my arms in triumph. Nothing to do with track ever felt like winning to me. After every single race, I was just filled with great relief that it was over. And this race wasn't any different. But what *was* different was that none of my teammates congratulated me or were happy that I'd won. My talents were not welcome on this team at all. Everyone out there wanted to be number one, and I was standing in the way of that. I wished so badly they could understand that I needed the win more than they wanted the win. For me, winning races meant keeping the peace at home. And that's all it meant.

I have to admit, though, that I was secretly satisfied with myself for kicking Cara's instigating, arrogant butt. And I found it even more satisfying that she switched race specialties after that day from the 400 meters to the 400 meter hurdles. And though we never went head to head again on the track, she never stopped finding ways to compete with me off the track.

Jolted back to reality by the obnoxious muffler sound coming from a souped-up Camaro in the student parking lot, I started to think more about what I'd just done, and anxiety consumed me. I had no idea how I was going to tell my dad that I'd quit track. I couldn't begin to put together a sentence in my head that I thought would spare me his wrath. I briefly entertained the thought of running away, but I quickly ruled that out because I lived in the middle of nowhere in farm country USA. Where would I go, and how would I get there? I had to accept there was no getting out of having to face the music on this one. Nothing could save me from the consequences of the decision I'd made. Nothing and no one.

I could see in the distance some of the soccer players leaving, which meant I still had an hour to sit there and wait on my Mom. As the soccer players filtered out, I couldn't help but wonder if there were any other kids in my school going through what I was. Any other kids here forced to play a sport, intimidated and pressured by a parent to compete and to win. Does any other kid here suffer the threat of physical consequences if they lose? It seemed so crazy. It was crazy, right? I wondered this all the time, but I never knew the answer because it's all I'd ever known.

My dad had cultivated the fear in me related to running as far back as I could remember. Several years prior, when I was only ten years old, he had one of his drinking buddies over to help him work on the farm. They started drinking Budweiser beer around eleven that Saturday morning and kept drinking well into the night.

Needless to say, I was worried all day for what that meant for Mom, Nate, and me. The three of us steered clear of them as best we could throughout the day. That night, I tried to stay awake so I could make sure my mom would be alright, but I drifted off to sleep sometime around midnight.

All of a sudden, I was awakened by someone banging on my bedroom door. I heard my Dad ranting and hitting the door, and my heart started to pound out of my chest.

"Open this damn door, now! I mean now, Jena! Don't make me fucking break it down!" my dad wailed.

Scared to death, I leaped across my bed and opened the door. As I stood there in my nightgown, my dad yelled at me to get some shorts and tennis shoes on and get out in the front yard. I didn't understand what was happening, but I knew better than to say a single word when he was this drunk and this mad.

I glanced at my clock and saw it was 2:20 a.m. I was suddenly petrified. Was this the night? I'd feared for years that one of us wasn't going to make it out alive during one of his drunken rages, but when you're actually faced with that potential moment, it's terrifying. I wondered if my mom was okay and where Nate was. No sooner had I finished that thought than I heard my mom's plea, "Please, Richard, just let her sleep, please!" Immediately following, I heard a loud crack, and I knew he'd just hit her. With the speed of light, I got the other shoe on and was at the front door, hugging my mom, who was holding her face in her hands and crying. My dad had already made his way back outside. Through her tears, she said, "You don't have to go, Jena. You can go back to sleep.

Go back to your room."

"No, Mom, it's okay. I'm okay. I'm not scared."

That must have been the millionth lie I'd told my mom of this nature over the years. But I just didn't want to make it worse for her. I didn't want her to be more afraid than she already was, and I wanted to protect her as best I could. My mom took the worst beatings of any of us, both physically and verbally. I looked past her now out the door to see what was waiting for me, and I saw my dad and his friend out there, as loud as they could be, yucking it up. When my dad spotted me at the front door, he yelled, "Jena, get your ass out here pronto!" I hugged Mom tightly for a few seconds more and then gently pushed past her to open the door. Even though it was summer, there was a chill in the air during the early morning hours, and goose bumps instantly blanketed my arms and legs.

"Get on out here, c'mon now, let's go!" My dad's appearance would remind you of a marine, with his jet-black hair in a tight military buzz cut, his chiseled face, and his strong muscular build. He's not all that tall at 5'11", but he seemed like a giant to me. His coal-black eyes matched his hair, which he'd had in a buzz cut as far back as I could remember. Right then, he looked like one very angry, very drunk marine.

"Now, Jena, you show Paul here how fast you are. Mmm-kay. I've been telling him that my daughter is like Jesse Owens, born with a heart murmur and faster than anyone!" His words were so slurred I could barely make out what he was saying. Instantly, I felt sick to my stomach, and a huge wave of panic set in. *Oh no, not this*, I thought. *Please God, not this.* What was wrong with him? Did he even hear the stuff that came out of his mouth? Jesse Owens? It was like my dad was trying to force some kind of greatness out of me so he could feel better about himself. Like he thought that if I did something great then he must be great because I'm his kid. It was an impossible amount of pressure he put on me. He acted like this running thing was life or death. And what was worse was he made me believe that too.

Next thing I knew, he jerked me up by the back of my neck and barked, "Pay attention when I'm talking to you, Jena! Now get your ass down here with me on this line!" I couldn't believe he was going to make me run on the wet grass in the middle of the night. With each step I took toward this imaginary line, I wanted to vomit. My dad finally let go of me, and as he shoved me toward this invisible starting line, he said, "Okay, now, we are going to start here on my call and run down past Paul. Understand me?"

My mom was still at the door, and I didn't want to do anything to put the focus back on her, so I reluctantly shook my head in agreement. The rumbling in my stomach was uncontrollable, and it hurt so badly, but I managed to push it back.

He started, "On your mark, set, go!" and we were flying. As we got down past Paul a handful of seconds later, I knew I had won. I was feeling relief that it was over and thought maybe my dad would let me go back inside now. Before I could even finish that thought, my head was jerked forward, and I felt a horrible stinging pain. My dad had slapped me so hard in the back of my head that it knocked me to the ground. My hands and knees slid across the wet grass, and I felt the skin on my knees burning. But I didn't dare cry. I didn't make a single sound.

"You jumped the line, you little shit! Don't you ever fucking cheat again! Parks don't cheat! We're winners! Not cheaters! Get your ass back down there and do it again the right way or I'll put a foot up your ass!"

God, you have to help me! Please! Can't you see me out here? Please see me. Pleeeeeaasse help me!

I had no idea what I was supposed to do now. Was I supposed to let him win? I could literally feel my heart beating, and I was so scared that my hands began to shake. As fear consumed me, I heard his drunken friend cackling as if he'd just seen the funniest thing.

God, I am never going to understand why you let this happen. Why do you let him get away with this? I know you can stop him. Please, God. Please make it stop. I can't take it anymore. I just want to go back inside. Pllllleeeeeaaassse!

All through my childhood, I never used a phrase more than that one. "Please, God. Make it stop. I can't take it anymore." And I never logged the kind of hours talking to people that I did talking to God. Though sometimes it felt like I was just talking at God because nothing ever changed. But I kept talking. I knew he was there. And I knew he was our only hope. Couldn't he see that one of us was going to die if he didn't do something? God couldn't possibly want that to happen.

But it was clear to me that God wasn't going to act in this moment. "Jena, get up off the fucking ground and back on this line right now!" I made my way back to this stupid imaginary line of my dad's as he screamed, "Mark, set, go!" This time I let him cross first but just by a hair. I kept my eyes glued to him, not about to turn my back on him again. This time he charged toward me, roaring, so angry he was spitting as he spewed words so loud and slurred I couldn't make them out.

I was so scared I felt like I was going to pee myself, so I squeezed my legs together and focused really hard on not letting that happen.

My dad grabbed a huge handful of my long brown hair and dragged me all the way back down to the starting line, screaming at me the whole way while I struggled to keep my feet under me so he didn't pull my hair out.

"I know you're not fucking stupid! You know what you're supposed to do! Now don't make me have to tell you one more time or you'll be sorry! You get your ass on this line, you don't jump the line, and you don't slow up at the end! You run a fair race and you run it as fast as you can. It's simple. Do you fucking understand me?"

I wanted so badly to scream, "No, I don't understand you! I don't even know what you want from me!" But I didn't say a word. I just screamed on the inside in total silence.

I was finally able to mutter, "But I don't know what you want me to do. I am running my best, and I didn't cheat." Before I could finish the word *cheat*, I felt the sting of his backhand across my wet check, and I fell to the ground again.

"But I don't know what to dooooo," he said in a whining voice, mocking me. "Quit crying, you big baby! Crying is for weaklings! Are you a weakling? No, you're not. Cry again and I'll give you something to cry about! Now get your ass up and let's get on with it! Now!"

Something inside me began to well up, something other than fear and tears. As I sat there muddy in the wet grass with bloody knees and a throbbing cheek, I became aware that I was suddenly so incredibly angry. It was bad enough when he beat on me and humiliated me when it was just the four of us, but this was a whole new low, even for my dad, hitting me in front of someone else. This anger overtook my fear, and I decided I'd had enough. I hadn't forgotten that I was physically weaker than him, helpless when it came right down to it. I never forgot that. But I could run. And he couldn't catch me.

During the beatings, anger often tricked me into believing that I had some control in the most powerless of situations. And even though it was an illusion, it felt better somehow. Safer. Enduring abuse and accepting it are two completely different things. I was forced to endure my dad's abuse, but I never accepted it. I was always toggling between two distinct emotions—fear and anger.

Back on my feet now and on this ever-changing starting line, all I could think as I looked over at him was, *If you touch me again, I'll make you chase me around this farm all night. Hopefully, I'll run you out in front of a truck, and I won't have to fear you ever again.*

"On your mark, set, go!" And I was gone. I crossed the finish line in the blink of an eye and just started walking toward the house. I glanced over at my dad, and he said, "Now see, that's all you had to do, Jena! That's my girl!" And he high-fived tweedle dumb.

When I got to the door, my mom grabbed me and held me so tight. She couldn't stop crying. "I'm so sorry. I'm so sorry, Jena."

"Mom, I'm okay. I'm just tired. Can I go to sleep now? Will you come with me?" I was so mentally and physically drained, but I knew I wouldn't be able to sleep if my mom wasn't with me. I had to know she was safe. And as bad as she felt for me, I felt worse for her. I knew it was agonizing for her that she couldn't stop him from hurting me. He beat her senseless when she tried. And that was the worst thing that could happen in my mind. I couldn't bear to see him striking her. I'd much rather take the brunt of it. I've always believed the beatings and degradation that she suffered in front of me harmed me far more than any direct abuse I suffered. It's what I saw him do to her all those years that broke me as a person.

Mom told me to change my clothes and wash up and that I could sleep on her floor beside her bed. And I understood that she couldn't sleep in my room with me. We both knew that if he came to bed and she wasn't in their room, it would be bad for her. Very bad. And my dad wouldn't see me over there on her side of the bed unless he went to the closet, which he pretty much never did until morning. I either snuck out before he woke up or slipped underneath the bed if I heard him get up when I was still in there.

While I was in the hall bathroom washing up in the sink, I thought that this was what we were always doing, trying to wash away and hide all of the evidence of the abuse we suffered at the hands of a madman. But why did we hide it? I didn't know. It just seemed like the natural thing to do. Hide it and pretend it had never happened.

I finished cleaning my knees with peroxide, which stung badly, and then covered the grass burns with Neosporin and Band-Aids.

I tossed my muddy clothes in the hamper and then stuck my head just slightly outside the bathroom door, trying to hear where my dad and his friend were before sneaking into my mom's room. I could still hear them outside, so I quickly scurried into her room and over to her side of the bed. My mom hugged me before climbing into bed, and I lay down on her floor and reached up and held her hand, making sure our hands met off the edge of the bed so my dad wouldn't see that I was there. It seemed like this was how I went to bed almost every night of my life, needing proof she was okay, that she was still alive. As I lay there trying to go to sleep, I was too tired to say my prayers, but I managed, *God, please, please end this nightmare we're living.* The tears flowed as I faded from sheer exhaustion.

I let out a deep breath and decided that all this reminiscing about my long and tortured history with running wasn't doing me any good, so I walked around to the front of the school to wait for my mom. Before I could get my backpack hoisted, I saw her little red Pontiac round the corner of the parking lot, and my stomach started doing flip-flops.

"Hi, Mom."

"Hi, Jena. How was your day?"

Our eyes met as I tossed my bag into the back and settled into the front seat. Her tone quickly changed. "Jena, what's going on? What's wrong?"

"Can we just start driving, Mom, and then I'll tell you? I just want to get out of here."

As we pulled from the back parking lot to the front of the school and onto the main road that headed out of town, my mom said, "Okay, now tell me, Jena, what?"

"I quit track today."

Dead silence. Deafening silence. Uncomfortable silence.

I knew we were both feeling the exact same thing. Fear. Mounting anxiety. Minds racing. My actions were going to start a war at home that none of us would be able to defend against.

God, I really don't understand the situation I'm in. I can't understand how a stupid sport can be so important. Why does it matter so much? Please don't let him hurt us because of what I did today. Please help me when he gets home. I really hope you're listening to me, God, because I'm so afraid of what he's going to do.

After what seemed like fifteen minutes or more, my mom finally said, "You're going to have to tell your dad, Jena." I could hear the distress in her voice.

"I know." That was all I could offer. I couldn't stand that I'd done something to cause my mom to be afraid. It felt horrible. How could I have been so selfish?

When was I going to tell my dad, I wondered. I knew I'd have to tell him before he left for work the next day because he'd be planning on coming to the track meet. If he showed up and found out I'd quit through someone else, he'd kill me for sure.

I didn't realize I'd had my eyes closed until I felt the car pull onto the gravel in our driveway. I glanced up as we rounded the circle and saw our flag waving on the flagpole, and I was momentarily caught up in its beauty. This flag was one of my dad's most prized possessions, and looking at it, I couldn't help but think about what a contradiction my dad was. Everything he said he cared about—country, God, family—every single thing that he said mattered to him was in direct opposition with his actions and the life he led. It didn't make sense to me. He was the biggest hypocrite to ever walk the earth, as far as I was concerned. And this huge, majestic American flag that waved in the center of our circular driveway was a daily reminder of his hypocrisy. Not that beating your wife and children means you're un-American, I guess, but it certainly made me wonder how he could see himself as this patriotic, God-fearing family man. When my dad got to talking about God, the tears just streamed down his face, and I had to walk away. I couldn't imagine God wanted anything to do with him or wanted my dad even claiming firsthand knowledge of him.

I must have gotten lost in that thought staring up at the flag because my mom said, "Jena, are you going to get out of the car?"

"Oh yeah, sorry, Mom. I'm coming."

I hesitated to walk in when she held the front door open for me, but I knew there was no other choice for me to make. I still had about an hour until my dad got home, so I headed down the hallway to my room, closed the door, and plopped facedown on my bed. I buried my face so deep in the pillow that everything went black as I tried my hardest to pretend I was nowhere and that I felt nothing. When I turned my head to the side to breathe, the bright sun that streamed through the window warmed my face, and I tried to force my mind into the moment of this simple pleasure: the sun on my face, the warmth of it and the comfort.

Within minutes, my stomach betrayed me as the anxiety took

over and I had to move. I jumped up, changed out of my practice clothes and into some jeans and a T-shirt, and headed outside.

My mom heard the door open and yelled from the kitchen, "Jena, where are you going?"

"Outside to ride my bike, Mom."

"Be back inside for dinner when your dad gets here!"

"I will." *Thanks for the reminder*, I thought to myself as a few more knots formed in my stomach. I jumped on my bike and headed down the driveway and turned left toward the big dirt hill at the bottom of the property where our road and Church Road intersected. This was the way my dad came home from work, and more times than not at this time of day, I could be found sitting high atop this dirt mound watching for his car to round the corner onto our road while pleading with God to not let him round that corner ever again. This was where I would go when I was trying to persuade God that my dad getting into a car accident, one where no one but him was hurt, was the best possible thing for everyone. I would make the argument that because he was God, he could even make it quick and painless. It's not like I wanted my dad to suffer; I didn't. I just wanted our suffering to stop.

No sooner had I finished pleading with God than I heard a car. Sure enough, it was my dad. To say I felt disappointed was a huge understatement. Frustrated and confounded was more accurate. Why did he get to keep living and keep hurting us? I just couldn't understand it. Especially when I knew that God could make him go away. How was that not the best possible option? I didn't get it. What was I missing that God was seeing?

As I slid down the dirt hill on my butt, my mind spun back into a reality I was not ready to face. How was I going to face him and tell him what I'd done? I leaped to the seat of my bike and raced the back way through the field to try to beat my dad into the driveway. I was able to pull behind the garage right before he turned into the driveway and hoped he hadn't seen me. I decided to wait it out and let him get into the house before I headed in.

I couldn't let him be in there with my mom more than a minute or two before I got in there. I needed to see if he'd been drinking and what kind of mood he was in. Plus, I'd forgotten to tell Mom to pretend like she didn't know what I'd done today at practice. That way he couldn't hold it over her head later that she knew and didn't immediately tell him when he walked through the door.

I snuck into the rec room through the breezeway as quietly as I could so I could listen at the door to try to assess what kind of shape he was in. I could hear him in the kitchen talking to my mom, who was making dinner, and he sounded like he'd probably just started drinking because I heard an upbeat, pleasant tone in his voice. This usually meant he'd had just enough to drink where he was starting to feel the effects of the alcohol but not enough to begin his descent.

I felt sick to my stomach, so anxious. But then again, when did I not feel this way? It was varying degrees of the same feeling, day after day. But that night if I had to rate this feeling on a scale of one to ten, ten being off the charts, then it was a solid ten. I literally could have vomited at any moment.

This seemed as good a time as any to interject myself into the conversation, so I stepped into the kitchen.

"Hey, Dad," I said, trying not to sound nervous.

"How's my track star doing today!" he exclaimed with a huge smile.

"I'm good. I'm hungry. What's for dinner, Mom?" I don't know why I said that. I wasn't hungry at all! I was way too nervous to eat. And of all the ways he could have greeted me, it had to be, "How's my track star?"

"Spaghetti. Why don't you go wash up and call Nate?" my mom said, trying to back me out of the conversation and away from the stove. I'm sure she could envision the pots and pans flying if I entered into this firestorm right now. And no one wanted to have burning hot pots and pans thrown their way.

"Sounds great, Mom. Okay, I'm going!" I was already halfway down the hall by the time I finished my sentence. I ducked into the bathroom and shut and locked the door. I sat down on the toilet seat, dropped my head into my hands, and said one more prayer. *God, please help me get through this dinner. And help me to know what to say to my dad about track. I don't know what I'm supposed to do right now. Please protect me, my mom, and Nate. Please let this be no big deal. Please, God.*

And with that, I took a deep breath and headed down the hall to the kitchen. The last thing I needed was to irritate him by being late to the dinner table. I rounded the corner into the kitchen and took my seat at the table which, lucky me, was right beside my dad. I'm sure that placement wasn't by accident, though I couldn't remember who made the seating assignments. Probably my dad. I was glad Mom was the furthest away from him, but I sure wished it were Nate that had to sit right next to him and not me.

Nate was far better than me at staying out of physical harm's way with my dad. He just knew how to avoid those situations better than I did. That of course didn't spare him from Dad's venomous verbal cruelty. My dad was far crueler to Nate verbally and mentally than he was to me.

My dad noticed that I hadn't put much of anything on my plate and said, "Jena, didn't you just tell your mom that you're hungry? And isn't this your favorite meal? What the hell are you doing? Put some food on that plate! You won't have the energy to run eating like a bird!"

"Okay," I complied as I tried to force a smile. I put another small helping of spaghetti on my plate. I guess that wasn't enough for my dad because he started loading my plate with garlic bread and salad too.

"There you go! Now eat up!"

"Thanks."

"All right then, let's eat!" he said as he started to dig in.

We all knew to wait for my dad to say we could start eating before taking the first bite or there were consequences, none of them good. We also had to wait for my dad to address us in conversation before we could start talking at the dinner table. The penalty for speaking without first being spoken to was pretty steep as well.

That night I was good with that program as there was nothing I wanted to say and nothing I wanted to be asked.

"So, Jena, what team are you up against tomorrow?" my dad inquired between bites of spaghetti.

I kept staring down at my plate, but I knew my face was turning every possible shade of red. I could feel it. My mind was going to explode and my face was on fire. I had to say something. I had to give an answer...and I didn't dare look left or right. I didn't want to see the fear on my mom's face right then. Was I really going to have to do this at the dinner table with everyone present?

"Jena! Pay attention when I'm talking to you! Who do you race tomorrow?" he repeated in an agitated tone.

"Ummm, I'm not sure. I think it's...I think. Umm, I...I'm not really sure...I think...Dad...I quit today."

It was as if lightening had struck. It happened so fast I didn't even realize I'd been hit until my plate landed on my head as I hit the floor. My dad had backhanded me so hard that I'd fallen back over my chair, landing with a huge crash as my head bounced off the floor. Before I could assess if I was okay, my dad jerked me up off the floor by my hair and dragged me down the hallway. He didn't say anything, but the force with which he dragged me down the hall said it all.

When we got to the doorway of my bedroom, he kicked the half-open door so hard that it bounced back off the wall at us. He forced it open with his knee as he dragged me into my room and flung me across the bed. My whole body went flying over top of the bed and off the other side onto the floor and only stopped when I banged into my dresser.

"You quit? Are you fucking kidding me? You don't fucking quit! You're a Parks and Parks don't quit! You have your ass ready to go at seven in the morning! I'll take you to school and we'll get this mess cleared up. You have a meet tomorrow! And don't you dare let me see your face outside of this room tonight! Do you hear me? I mean it! Stay out of my sight!"

He slammed my door shut so hard I thought it would break in two.

My immediate concern was that he was going to hurt my mom or Nate. *God, please, don't let him do that!* The anticipation of it was more than I could take, so I quickly got up and darted for my door, but when I tried to turn the knob it wouldn't turn. What was going on?

Unexpectedly, the door flew open and knocked me into the wall with such force I buckled to the ground.

"What the fuck did I just tell you? Not to let me see your face again tonight! Are you hard of hearing? You don't need to concern yourself with anything that happens outside this door! It's none of your fucking business! You stay in here and think about what you've done! Now get up!" He kicked the side of my thigh hard before slamming the door once more.

I didn't move. My leg hurt so badly I wasn't sure that I could move. I just sat there and cried so hard that I couldn't breathe, and I couldn't see through all the tears. I cried for so long that the hair in front of my face was matted and soaked. I felt numb and unable to gather my thoughts. I tried to focus on the carpet, the thickness of it and the softness of it on my cheek, the color of it, how white it was.

Next thing I knew, I woke up, still on the floor and so alarmed. How long had I been sleeping? Oh my gosh, what about my mom? And Nate? Were they okay? My heart started pounding. I got up off the floor and looked at the alarm clock beside my bed; it said 9:12 p.m. I felt a sharp pain in my thigh, and I could feel a knot where my dad had kicked me. I leaned over to the door and put my ear up against it to see if I could hear anything. Nothing. I had to know if my mom was okay—I had to know! But I was so afraid to open the door. If he heard me or saw me, it was over.

God, please, tell me what to do! I have to know if they are okay. I have to!

I kept my ear pressed to the door, straining to hear any sounds at all. Nothing. Not even the sound of Nate's music, which I could almost always hear through the house. I was panicking because after five minutes with my ear pressed tightly to the door, I still couldn't hear a sound. *God, you know I have to open this door. So please protect me when I do. I need to know if they are okay.* Nate and I had to be in our rooms by nine o'clock sharp every night. Mom and Dad would sometimes go into their room then but more often than not, they would wait until ten. I figured that Nate was already in his room, so I got inside my closet and pressed my ear to the wall between his room and mine. Still nothing. Not a sound. Maybe he was already asleep.

But what about my mom? I reasoned with myself that even if he caught me, the beating wouldn't be too severe because he planned on making me go to school with him tomorrow and wouldn't want to leave any visible marks on me. But that didn't mean he wouldn't punish my mom for it. In fact, that would be just like him because he knew that would hurt me more. That's how he knew that I was going to try to come out of my room earlier. He knew I'd have to know what happened to Mom and Nate. It was imperative that I be really careful and really quiet when I opened the door.

I strained to hear any sounds a little while longer until I just couldn't take not knowing any longer. Slowly, and as quietly as I could, I twisted my doorknob and very cautiously opened the door, praying that it didn't creak. Once it was open far enough to see that my mom and dad's door was closed, I opened it all the way.

What did I do now? There was no way they were sleeping this early. I peered down the hall and saw that all of the lights were off in the house. So they must be in their bedroom. I couldn't just go to bed. What if he had killed her while I was sleeping? And it would be all my fault. *God, you have to help me! I have to know if Mom and Nate are okay!* Pure desperation is what I felt.

I had to open their bedroom door too, and this made my stomach churn. I knew what a reckless idea this was, but I didn't have any other options. I took as quiet a step as I could outside of my room into the hallway and then froze and listened. Nothing. So I took another step. One more and I'd be at their door. As I took the last step, I carefully rested my hand and then my head against their door, trying to hear any sounds. Nothing. In very slow motion, I got to the floor and looked underneath the door to see if I could see any lights on. None. It was dark.

I didn't like my head being on the floor right outside his door in case he was waiting to pounce, so I got to my feet as quickly and quietly as I could. I put my hand around their doorknob and turned it just a little bit. It wasn't locked. So what now, I wondered? Did I turn it all the way and open the door? My dad was literally three or four steps inside this door, and he faced the door when he slept.

It was a huge risk. If he was awake, I was cooked. I already had it halfway turned. My heart raced, wondering if he'd already seen the doorknob turning and was just waiting to attack me when I opened the door. I braced for it to happen, turned the knob all the way, and pushed on it slightly. The door creaked! I froze.

Shit! My heart dropped into my stomach. I was in it now, though, so I had to keep going. I pushed the door open a little further and saw it was dark inside. I could see them lying in bed. I was so scared, and the adrenaline was pumping through me like crazy. It would be just like my dad to fake being asleep and jump up and scare me half to death. My eyes adjusted to the darkness, and I could see that he was out. I could hear in his labored breathing that he wasn't pretending. I saw a glass of whiskey beside him on his nightstand and could smell it permeating the room. I tried to focus past him on my mom to make sure she was okay, but I couldn't really tell. I decided to sneak past him to her side of the bed, which I knew was risky because if he awakened, there was no way out for me but through him. But I also knew I wouldn't be able to sleep until I knew for sure that Mom was okay.

I wondered if I should get low to the ground and belly crawl over to her side like I usually did when I checked on her or keep standing and walk over there. Crawling was quieter, but I would be more vulnerable on the floor if he woke up and caught me. I took a step into their room and decided to walk around their bed to check on her. It seemed like it took me ten minutes to go ten steps, but I was so afraid the floor would creak so I'd pause for a minute between each step before taking another. Finally, I was on my mom's side. She was facing away from my dad, so I could see her face now, but I still couldn't tell if she was breathing, so I knelt down and got closer. I didn't want to wake her up and scare her, which would wake my dad up. I'd often feared my dad mistaking me for an intruder when I was doing this and shooting me dead. But my fear of that wasn't as great as my fear that he'd harmed my mom. I very slowly reached my hand out in front of her nose to try to feel her breath. And I did.

Thank you, God! My relief was immediate. I wished I could see her more clearly to see if she had any bruises or cuts, but I knew that wasn't possible, and I settled for knowing she was still alive. Now I had to make my way back out of there without being caught. It took me another ten minutes at least, but I made it out and was able to close the door without alerting anyone that I was there. Instead of going straight back to my room, I headed down the hall the other way and opened Nate's door. I almost jumped out of my skin when I heard him toss in his bed and angrily whisper, "Shut my door!" I didn't blame him, though. Tonight was all my fault, and whatever stress, anxiety, and abuse Mom and Nate suffered while I slept on my floor would be on my shoulders. I had done this.

I closed Nate's door as quietly as I could and headed back to my room, where I shut and locked my door. I always locked my door for fear my dad would come in during the night and hurt me. I wanted to at least be able to hear him coming. I got in trouble for this all the time. My dad said I couldn't lock the door in case there was a fire and they needed to get me out, but I'd rather take my chances with the fire than him. I could always get out through one of my two windows if there was a fire. But our locks were very easily opened. All you had to do was break the head of a Q-tip off and push it through the tiny round hole in the locking mechanism and the lock popped open. I did it all the time when my dad locked me out of their bedroom at night.

He did this especially when he was abusing my mom. He knew I was coming in regardless; the locked door never stopped me. Neither did his yelling to me, "Jena, you stay the fuck out of here! Don't you dare open that fucking door or you'll be sorry!" But I never was. Sorry. Even though going in guaranteed a surefire beating, I knew it lessened the one my mom was getting. I would put myself in between them and take a lot of the blows he'd otherwise land on her. Once I was taller than my mom, it was hard for him to reach her cleanly around me. And when he threw me aside, I'd just get right back in there. When all else failed, I'd wrap my whole body around one or both of his legs and hinder his ability to get ahold of my mom.

You'd be surprised how used to the physical abuse you become. The physical blows aren't what destroy you. It's the fear of the blow. Because you know it's coming. You don't know when. You don't know where, and you don't know how. But you know that it's coming. And the looming anticipation of it consumes every waking moment of every day. It's agony living in a constant state of fear. And it makes it impossible to function normally. Surprisingly, the calmest you ever feel is during the attacks because your mind and your body shift simultaneously into survival mode. There's no time for fear and anxiety while you're fighting for your life or for the life of someone you love.

Trauma: Complex or no? Ⓐ

Chapter 3
No Reprieve

Back in my bed, I was incredibly restless thinking about what would happen the next morning when my dad dragged me into school. I was sure his plan was to see my track coach and force me back onto the team. I prayed that Coach White said no. There might be hell to pay for me for a while at home, but I just couldn't go back to that round-the-clock fear and pressure. I just couldn't do it. Maybe finally my coach would get what I'd been going through all those years and save me.

All too soon, my alarm clock started buzzing. I wasn't ready. I thought, *Please let there be a few more hours to sleep.* Though I rarely fell asleep out of anything other than sheer mental, physical, and emotional exhaustion, I loved sleeping all the same because it was the only time I could escape from my life. And though most of my dreams were nightmares, it was still far better than my waking hours.

Bang! Bang! Bang! I was jolted to a sitting position by the heavy banging on my door. "Get up, Jena!" my dad yelled. "We are leaving in thirty minutes. Don't make me wait on you!"

If it were possible to just disappear, I would have given anything to be able to do that right then. I couldn't believe I had to do this. And with him. I got to my feet and glanced in my dresser mirror to see if I had a mark on my face from his backhand at the dinner table. Unfortunately, I didn't. Normally, I would have been thankful there was no evidence of his abuse on my face so I didn't have to explain it away, but not this day. I was hoping for some black and blue or swelling or something that would allow me to stay home and dodge whatever my dad had in store for me at school. I noticed that my leg was incredibly sore, so I pulled down my jeans, which I had slept in all night, and, sure enough, I had an enormous deep-purple bruise on my upper thigh. I grabbed my track shorts to check if it would show, and you could definitely make out the bottom edge of the bruise. *Good*, I thought, which again was an unusual way for me to be thinking. It's not like I could actually admit where it came from, but at least if he forced me back onto this team then maybe my coach would start to piece together why I hated this sport so much, and maybe he'd kick me off the team to help me out. Because that bruise definitely wasn't there at practice yesterday. And it was massive.

As I finished brushing my hair in the bathroom mirror and putting on some light makeup, I looked at the girl staring back at me and thought, *What kind of life is this you live? Can you remember even one day you didn't go to bed afraid and wake up afraid?* I felt like I should look a hundred years old, but the youthful reflection staring back at me masked the truth. *Please, God, please, don't let the coach take me back on the team. Please give me this one thing. Just this one thing.*

My mind wandered to the place it often did, a place of utter frustration and confusion as to why God didn't seem to ever answer my prayers the way that I wanted him to. The way that I needed him to. *Why am I not angry with you, God? I know that you exist. I know that you see everything that happens. I know you hear my prayers. I know that you can stop my dad from ever raising a hand to us again. I am certain of all of these things. So why am I not mad at you for not doing anything to help us? It doesn't make any sense. I should be mad at you, God, really mad. When are you going to make it stop?*

"Jena! Come on! Now!" My discussion with God was abruptly interrupted as my dad summoned me from the other end of the house. Nothing like being jolted back to reality by my dad's voice.

One thing is for sure, God, if I didn't have you to talk to, I would lose my mind. You are the only one I can talk to in this whole world. And I love you even though you never answer my prayers. Will you pleeeeeaaaase just consider on the ride to school not letting my coach take me back on the team?

As I walked to the front door, my mom headed me off and hugged me. She told me that she loved me. I couldn't speak or I'd cry, but I knew she understood.

I stepped out into the brisk morning air and took a deep breath. My dad was already in his prized company car, a long, sleek brown Buick. I never knew which seat to sit in, but I assumed he'd want me sitting up front today, so I plopped myself down in the seat and settled in with an enormous sense of doom. I had so many butterflies in my stomach, and the overbearing smell of my dad's Old Spice was not helping matters.

The first few minutes were so quiet. No radio. Nothing. But

then it started...

"Now, when we get there, Jena, you let me do the talking. We all know he needs you on that team, but I'm sure he's not happy with you storming out of practice. When you are the best, Jena, you can't do things like that. People take it the wrong way. He probably thinks you think you're too good to be on his team. Which, let's face it, you are. But that's beside the point. You just keep your mouth shut, and I'll handle your coach. And let me tell you something, you better never pull this kind of shit again. Do you understand me?"

"Yes," I mumbled in my autopilot response tone. I mean, when had I ever been able to answer how I really wanted to answer? I don't know why he even asked me questions. He never got real answers. Just the ones I was forced to give.

"Yes, what?"

"Yes, I understand." Why did I do this? I knew exactly what he wanted me to say...yes, sir. It was that thing deep inside of me that I couldn't always push down. That thing that wanted to show him that he didn't own me.

"Yes, what!" he said angrily as he slapped the steering wheel.

"Yes, sir," I said with a hint of sarcasm. Though it bugged me so much to say it, I reminded myself that it didn't mean anything if he had to force it out of me. It's not like it was a sincere response. And I knew he knew that. Somehow, that made me feel better.

I just wanted him to be quiet and leave me alone so I could panic in silence. I knew he wasn't going to hit me because he couldn't take a chance of leaving a mark. It was these rare moments I relished, when he and I both knew he couldn't strike me because he had something to lose. Usually it was just Nate, Mom, and me that had something to lose.

I looked out my window the rest of the car ride, trying to force myself to tune in to the farm fields we were passing and all the animals behind the fences. I liked living in the country. I liked the smell of the fresh air and the sounds the birds made and even the crickets at night. I liked how I knew who lived in almost every house we passed. As we came up on the huge white Victorian farmhouse on Fitzhugh Road, I saw Lisa's brand-new Trans Am parked in her driveway, and my mind shifted to the story she'd shared in English class the first day of school this year.

We were each asked to stand in front of the class and talk about one fun thing we'd done that summer. Lisa's family had spent four weeks in Hawaii, and while I hung on every detail of her incredible vacation, I couldn't imagine it as a reality. Certainly not my reality anyway. We had never taken a family vacation. And it was funny to me that I'd never even wondered why until that day sitting there listening to Lisa talk about her summer adventure.

The classes where we were asked to share something about ourselves or our lives were the toughest for me. I never had anything to say, so I always made something up, especially when we had to talk about what we had planned for the future. I never considered that I had a future, so it really never occurred to me to think beyond the present day. I couldn't relate to the kids that had their lives all planned out. It seemed completely foreign to me. I was always just praying to make it to the next day.

When we made the turn that led over the covered bridge at the end of Fitzhugh, my stomach started churning, and all too soon we pulled into the school parking lot. Thankfully, we were early. The buses hadn't started to arrive yet, and hardly any cars were in the student parking lot. I didn't even know if the front door was open. I'd never been here this early.

"Let's go," he said as he exited the car.

I followed him down the sidewalk to the front entrance as he pulled one of the big green doors open.

"Which way to your coach, Jena?"

"This way." I pointed as I took the lead.

Oh, God, please don't let him be here, and if he is, please don't let my dad embarrass me! Please don't let him cuss. And thank you that at least he didn't drink anything this morning. Please just make it so I don't have to run track anymore! Thanks, God.

As we turned down the hall where my coach's classroom was, the anxiety was almost more than I could stand. I paused outside his door and just pointed in its direction to my dad. I didn't want to go in there first.

But my dad didn't hesitate. He walked right in, and I tried to hide behind him as best I could.

"Morning, Mr. White." My dad extended his hand. Coach White shook my dad's hand but didn't do a very good job hiding the smug look on his face. It was as if he had been expecting us.

"What can I do for you, Mr. Parks?" he said, pretty much ignoring my presence, which was fine by me. By all means, please act like I am not here. That would be pretty close to accurate anyway.

"Well, I understand that Jena got upset in practice yesterday and left before it was over. She's here to apologize for that. She knows I don't tolerate quitting in our family. And I know her actions really hurt the team, as they depend on her points. So I brought her in this morning so we can clear this whole thing up. I assure you she won't pull that again. Jena, what do you have to say to Mr. White?"

My dad's intense glare went to waste as I refused to look in his direction. I could feel it, though. I knew it was there. *What do I have to say?* I thought. *Me? I've got nothing to say. This wasn't my idea.* How I wished I had the guts to say that out loud. But I didn't.

"Umm. Sorry," I mumbled.

"For what, Jena?" I could tell my dad was losing his patience with me, but that was the least of my worries. He was trying to get me back into something that forced me to live in a constant pressure cooker. And I didn't want to do it.

My coach was staring at me with that arrogant expression of his.

"Jena!" my dad practically yelled.

"I'm just sorry," was the best I could do.

Before my dad could chastise me again for not expressing myself exactly the way he wanted me to, Coach White jumped in.

"Jena, I don't even know what you were so upset with yesterday. Can you tell me?"

"I don't know. I just didn't feel good."

"Are you sick, Jena? Because I can understand that. But what is hard to understand is why the best runner on the team behaves that way. Don't you know that because of your talent, you have a responsibility to your team to lead by example? Others look up to you. If I allow that kind of prima donna behavior out of you, it sends the wrong message to the rest of the team. I can't have them thinking that you get preferential treatment because of your talent. That just wouldn't be fair. Do you understand?"

I'm not sure I had ever been so speechless. *Prima donna* behavior? Had he really just called me a prima donna? He didn't have a clue who I was! I was the kid who was so damn afraid of breathing the wrong way that I couldn't even think straight. I was the kid who was so afraid to lose a stupid race because my drunk-ass father would beat me senseless that I threw up before every race! I was *that* kid. I wanted to scream all of that at him so badly. But I just kept looking down at the floor so that I was able to contain myself. *God, please let his next words be that because of my prima donna behavior, he just can't have me back on the team. Please let that be his next sentence!*

"I'll tell you what, Jena. Why don't we try to forget yesterday even happened. Let's wipe the slate clean and start over. Sound good?"

No! It didn't sound good. I was dying inside! That sounded like a horrible idea! I couldn't believe this was happening. *God, where are you? Where?*

My Dad nudged my shoulder to respond. I didn't. I just kept looking at the floor.

"That sounds fair, Mr. White. Thank you for your time. Come on, Jena."

But as my dad tugged on my shoulder to head toward the door, Mr. White wasn't quite finished trying to make me eat humble pie.

"Wait. Please. Jena? I'm willing to start over if you are. What do you say?"

I glanced up and nodded. It was all I could manage. Not a chance he was ever going to save me. Not for a minute. Coach was always going to do what was in his own best interest. There would be no reprieve for me, and it was the worst feeling in the world. I felt completely defeated as the tears welled up in my eyes. I tried not to let either one of them see me crying, but Coach White noticed.

"Come here, kiddo," he said as he gave me a hug. "Everything's forgiven, don't worry. Okay?"

I wanted to weep. Weep at how absurd this whole thing was! All is forgiven? By whom?

All is forgiven?

I got so lost in thought that I barely noticed my dad and I were back out in the hall. When we got about ten steps further down he said, "What the hell was that back there?"

And I hoped he was referring to the absurdity of everything the coach had just said.

"Jena, what kind of apology was that?" he said half irritated and half laughing, like he was mad but also proud that I hadn't fallen all over myself apologizing to the coach.

"I just don't like him," I offered matter-of-factly.

"Well, I don't give two tiddlywinks who you do or don't like. It's not about him. You get your head on straight. You have a meet later today. I've got to get to work, but I will see you there."

No hug. No nothing. He just left me standing there.

Definitely no one sees me, God. No one sees the torture in my existence. No one but you. And you did nothing to help me in there. Nothing. You could have so easily made my coach say no, and it would have been such a huge burden off of me. Why won't you help me? I try to be a good person. I take up for my mom all the time. I pray all the time. Well, I talk to you all the time. I think that's praying. And the only really bad thoughts I have are about my dad, and I think he deserves every bad thing I wish on him. What's wrong with me, God, that you won't help me? At least help my mom. She's the best person of any of us. It must hurt you to see her so abused.

Please just answer me! Even if you won't change things, make me understand why. It's too hard to live this way, always afraid and never with any peace. I'm exhausted, God, and I can't keep doing it.

"Jena! I don't think you've heard a word I've said, have you?" my homeroom teacher said, completely exasperated.

"Sorry, Ms. Gordon. I didn't hear you." I must have roamed the halls on autopilot to arrive at my homeroom class and take my seat without really focusing on where I was or what I was doing.

"Well, I know that, Jena. I called your name at least three times while looking right at you. Pay attention!"

As she moved past my desk to the back of the room, I let out a deep sigh. I'd been holding my breath and hadn't realized it. *God, I feel like just sitting here and talking to you all day, but I'm in enough trouble. Please help me to focus because I'm really not here. I'm anywhere but here. I'm nowhere.*

That entire day felt like I was in the twilight zone, like my body was present but my mind was nowhere to be found. I was sleepwalking through the day. I was even more agitated than usual, and I guess it got away from me in my third period English class. As Ms. Stanton was at the front of the class discussing a book the class had just read, I noticed two of my least favorite people whispering and gesturing at me. I knew they were talking about me. What's new? It was one of their favorite pastimes. Funny how they'd only do that during class and only if they were together. One-on-one they ran for the hills if they saw me coming. Cowards. I didn't usually waste my time or energy on them because they really didn't exist in my world, but today I just couldn't seem to let their badgering roll off of me. I could feel the anger growing inside me, and I tried to force my thoughts in a different direction.

Jena, they aren't worth it, I reminded myself. *I mean, who cares what they think, what they say? You're not friends with them. You don't want to be friends with them.* I kept trying to reason with myself, but I'd lost all track of what the teacher was saying, and I was fully tuned into Leanne and Hannah taunting me, almost daring me to say something. I was sitting in between two of my best friends, Eric and Samantha, and both of them could tell I was irritated. Eric kept trying to distract me from Leanne and Hannah's taunts. Samantha wrote on my notepad, "To hell with them, they're so jealous, just let it go. Ignore them. Teach is staring at you."

I glanced up at Ms. Stanton, and she was giving me that serious pay-attention-to-me look. It was a momentary distraction from the immature wenches sitting across from me, but then I heard Hannah laugh and say, "Think she can get that hair any bigger?" and I lost it, right there in the middle of class.

"What did you say?" I yelled across the room, glaring right at her. "Are you talking about me? Then have the guts to say it to me!" Dead silence throughout the classroom and Hannah's face turned bright red. "Oh, what, you have nothing to say now that you have my attention?"

Ms. Stanton slammed her book down on her desk. "Jena! Out in the hall. Now!"

I looked at Samantha as I slid out of my chair, and I could tell she was fighting back laughter, which in turn made me laugh. I couldn't help it. I hadn't even felt like anything was funny until I saw her fighting to contain herself. And I just started laughing. So Samantha started laughing, and then Eric was laughing, though he was working really hard to hide it. Eric never ever got in trouble, and I could tell he didn't want to now, either.

As I stepped into the hall with Ms. Stanton, she slammed the door behind us, and I could tell she was furious with me.

"Jena, what in God's name was that about? I've never seen you act like this. You're usually very quiet in class. Listen, young lady, this is my classroom, and no one makes an outburst like that in my class! No one. What is wrong with you? What happened in there? Tell me something that will change my mind about sending you to see the principal."

"I'm sorry, Ms. Stanton. I really am. I'm sorry for interrupting your class. I don't know what happened. I'm just having a horrible day, and usually I can ignore them when they start digging at me, but today I just couldn't sit there and take it. I tried to. But…"

"Jena, I've watched different groups of girls dig at you all year. It's nothing new. You know how some girls are. Catty. Mean. You're better than that. You know what's going on. I expect you to rise above the drama and conduct yourself like a lady. Today you let them bring you down to their level. Don't you know they win when you do that? You may have embarrassed them, but they got a rise out of you. And it landed you in trouble, not them. And you can believe they're happy about that!"

"I know. You're right. I just…I've had enough. You know? I get tired of people coming at me for no reason. I didn't do anything to them. Not just today, but ever. I am so sick of it." I could feel the tears fill my eyes. I was so sick of this feeling too, so sick of always being on the verge of crying.

Ms. Stanton sensed I was struggling and rested her hand on my shoulder. "I understand, Jena, I really do. But I can't allow that kind of behavior in my class. You understand that, right? And if you react this way every time someone says something about you that you don't like, you'll be fighting all the way through high school. What's the point of that? Just ignore them. Okay?"

"Okay. I'll try."

"Not try. Do! Okay, let's go back in." She waved her hand toward her classroom.

I followed Ms. Stanton back into the classroom and prayed that Samantha and Eric had gotten control of their laughter because I knew that if they hadn't and I took one look at them, it would start all over again. I managed to get through the rest of class without saying another word, but as soon as we hit the hall, Samantha started laughing and carrying on about me calling them out in front of everyone. Eric just shook his head and said, "You are extra tense today, Jena, what gives? And stop encouraging her, Samantha, she's not you!" I looked ahead and noticed Leanne and Hannah scurrying down the hall as quickly as they could without being obvious that they were trying to get out of my verbal reach.

I was so thankful I had study hall next period. The teacher didn't care what we did in there. I was definitely going to put my head down on my desk and hope I fell asleep. I didn't even care if someone had to wake me when the period was over. I just wanted to pretend I wasn't there, even if it was just for fifty minutes.

As I laid my head down on the cold surface of my desk, I thought about what had just happened in Ms. Stanton's class. I thought about how all those years of taking the abuse at home, just taking it over and over and not being able to stop it, how it does something to you. How it changes you. It sets the default switches way deep inside, so deep you can't reach them. It shapes the way you think, the way you act and react, especially when faced with conflict. And because silence is a staple of abuse, no one in the outside world knows what you're going through, so they can't begin to understand you. And let's face it, it's hard to be empathetic without understanding. Hard to be compassionate when your perception is so misconstrued.

People at school thought I had this great life. I heard, Jena you're so lucky because of this or you're so lucky because of that. And I never responded because it just made me want to cry. They had no idea how hard my life was. And some of them mistook my aloofness for arrogance. It was ludicrous; you'd have to actually feel good about yourself to be arrogant. They couldn't possibly know that I was just hanging on by a thread most days, trying to make it through each day without falling apart.

And when people came at me like Leanne and Hannah, it just sent me further inside myself, deeper into isolation. These things impacted me more than they should have. I was smart enough to know there were all kinds of conflicts in high school. But because of what I dealt with at home, it just hit me so much harder. When you've been stripped of your dignity for so long, the last thing you're going to do is allow another kid to bully you.

It was a double-edged sword; I had a need to be understood, and I wanted to fit in, but I was unwilling to let anyone know what I was going through. Most days I came to the conclusion that it was better for my classmates to mistake me for arrogant than to know how horrible my life really was. Ultimately, two things ensured my silence about the life I lived—shame and the fear that telling anyone could have fatal side effects.

I was just going to have to accept that high school was going to be a very lonely place for me. And I'd have to get through it the best way that I could.

Chapter 4

The Picnic

While my young life was consumed by daily mental, emotional, and physical abuse, there was one incident that rocked me to my core. It was the moment that broke me as a person and the thing that led to the extreme lack of trust I have for others. Considering the severity of the physical abuse we suffered at the hands of my dad for so many years, I think it will be surprising what affected me so profoundly.

As mornings went in the Parks household, this one wasn't as bad as most because the night before my dad hadn't gone off on any of us. He hadn't even gotten that drunk, and no one got hit. I thought it was because he was always in a pretty good mood when his annual company picnic rolled around, and this was the day. Even though I always thought it was pretty weird that my dad never took my mom, Nate, or me to this event, I have to admit that it was a day I looked forward to. My dad would be gone all day on a Saturday, which meant Nate and I had eight to ten hours that we knew we'd be okay and could enjoy doing normal, fun things with Mom. We lived for these rare occasions when we felt free. Free from fear, free from the threat of pain and suffering, free from being belittled, free to just breathe. I won't say we could fully relax because I never felt fully relaxed a single day of my childhood. Anxiety was a staple of my existence. But still, these precious hours when we could be together without him around were such a welcome gift.

My mom was in the kitchen packing up all of the food she'd made the day before for my dad to take to his picnic. Every year she made the majority of the food for the picnic. My mom was the best wife, the best mom, and it made me so sad that she was stuck living this life where she was so mistreated and taken for granted. My dad treated her like his property and made her work so hard. My mom did everything around our house: cooked, cleaned, tended the garden, mowed the lawn, painted, fixed things around the house when they broke, and drove us kids everywhere we needed to go. All he did was go to work, drink, and beat on us verbally and physically. That was literally all he did.

I was in the kitchen trying to help my mom pack the food when I heard my dad coming down the hall and immediately tensed up. Mom did too, but we were both pretty good at continuing on with whatever we were doing, thinking if we didn't look panicked then we might skate through without anything bad happening. My dad loved to magnify our fear when he could see or sense it in us. He was just cruel that way. So we continued talking to each other as he entered the kitchen, no doubt to make sure we were doing everything to his liking. As he took inventory of all of the food items, he nodded his approval but never once thanked her. I had to bite my tongue not to pipe up and thank her myself. How could he be on us all the time about manners and having to always say yes, sir; please; and thank you when he never did? All the things that my mom did for him and for all of us, and he never ever thanked her! I realized how mad I was getting, so I quickly reminded myself that he was about to leave and that I shouldn't waste any of this day even thinking about him.

And then, as if it was the most natural notion in the world, he leaned on the counter and said to my mom, "I think I'll take the kids with me today." I hadn't seen that coming. I mean, what in the world? He never took any of us. Why was he taking me and my brother but not my mom? I was instantly suspicious and nervous. Not so much that I was nervous to go with him. I mean, my brother would be there too, and I didn't think today would be the day he killed us and buried us in the yard like he was always threatening to do if Mom left him. No, this mood felt different. Like he was actually happy to be taking us. I didn't get it. And I could tell by the look on my mom's face that she didn't get it either. But I knew my mom would never tell my dad no about anything. What he said, went. We could choose the hard way or the excruciating way, but it would always be his way.

I stared at the floor because I didn't want him to see that I had absolutely no interest in going with him. I didn't want to make him lose his temper and ruin his otherwise good mood. He yelled for my brother, who was still in his room, no doubt waiting for Dad to leave before making an appearance. "Coming!" he said. He wouldn't challenge my dad, either. He preferred to just steer clear of him as much as possible. If I'd had any functioning brain cells, I would have done the same, but there was just something in me that wouldn't let me do that. I had to help my mom when everything went bad.

"Go get dressed. You and your sister are coming to the picnic with me today," my dad told him.

"Okay!" my brother said with a smile. I wondered if Nate was hiding his real feelings to avoid provoking Dad or if he was actually happy to be going. He couldn't be. Could he? Nate headed back down the hall to get dressed, and though I was hesitant to leave Mom alone with Dad, I quickly ducked into my brother's room to see if he was as worried about this idea as I was.

"I don't want to go, do you?" I questioned.

"Yeah, I want to go. You don't have to. Why don't you just stay with Mom? It's a bunch of guys at a lumber yard, why would you go?" I could tell he didn't want me anywhere near this event; he wanted time alone with Dad.

"I definitely want to stay with Mom, but if I say that and he gets mad and takes it out on Mom or us, then what? I don't know what to do." He knew I was right, so he reluctantly agreed. His fear of Dad's reaction outweighed his desire to not have me there.

I had been so excited to have time on a weekend with my mom without him around, and now I was anxious and worried that something was up, and that "something" wasn't good. The nagging thought that kept plaguing me was, what if my dad was going to send someone to our house to kill my mom while we were gone? Then he wouldn't be blamed for it because he would have an alibi.

He was making Nate and me a part of that alibi. The more that thought rattled around inside my head, the more consumed by it I became. So much so, I blurted out to my dad, "Why don't I just stay and help Mom with the chores today? You guys can go." His face tensed up, and he glared at me and said, "Be ready to leave by the time I get this cooler loaded into the car, Jena, understand?"

"Yes," I muttered.

Once my dad began loading the car, my mom came back to my bedroom and tried to ease my fears. "Honey, you'll have fun at the picnic. It will be alright."

I could feel the tears forming, and they began to fall. I said, "But will you be alright here without me?" She pulled me into her and hugged me tightly. "Jena, don't worry about me. I'll be just fine. I have a lot of work to do, and I'll have a really nice dinner ready for you when you get home, okay?" I couldn't tell if she was nervous about anything or had any horrible suspicions like I did.

"Okay, well, just keep all the doors locked, Mom," I insisted.

"Don't worry, I'll be fine. You go and have fun today."

My brother was already in the car in the front seat with Dad when I shuffled out the door. I hopped in the backseat, and my dad promptly headed out of the driveway. Something was so different about him that day. He was talking nicely to us going down the road and even joking with Nate. I couldn't figure it out, but I knew him well enough to know something was up. And the nicer he was to us, the more worried I got. Trying to think about something else or calm my nerves was a waste of time; I was never able to get there. So I just gave into total meltdown anxiety and suffered in silence all the way down the road. I tried to force a few smiles when he looked at me through the rearview mirror, but I felt like throwing up right there in his car. I couldn't believe my brother was so excited about this. How could he not know our dad well enough to know that something was really, really wrong? He had never been this nice to us or allowed any of us to come to this thing, let alone seemed so happy to have us there. No, uh-uh, I wasn't buying it. I knew better. A snake was still a snake whether it was sleeping or awake. And it could strike at any time. That was my dad. And I wasn't fool enough to forget it.

It seemed like the longest trip in the world, but according to the clock in the dash, we arrived in just a half an hour. We pulled into the lumberyard and up to my dad's office. I could see a lot of cars there and people carrying food in and out of the building. I wondered if the picnic was inside or outside. I preferred outside, wide-open spaces where I could run if I needed to.

"Okay, guys, we're here, everyone out of the car and wait for me to get the cooler. Alright, let's go." As he led the way across the parking lot and into his office, I heard a booming voice say, "Well, lookie what we have here, oh my! How are you two doing? What a nice surprise!" Elmer belted out from across the room. I could tell he was genuinely surprised we were there but also really happy to see us. "Come on over here, you two, and look what I have on my desk!" We looked at my dad for approval, and he nodded, so we ran over to see what Elmer had. There was a big bowl of candy bars on his desk. While any other time I would be thrilled at the offer of candy, my stomach was still doing cartwheels, and I knew I couldn't eat anything yet. But I didn't want to ruin Elmer's surprise, so I took one and said thank you. "Aww, come on now, you can hold more than that, can't you? Get in there and get you some good candy!" So we both took two candy bars. "Do I get a hug?" he teased. Elmer was an African American man probably in his 50s, and he had to be the nicest man I'd ever met. As I wrapped my arms around him, he gave me a big squeeze. My mom sometimes brought us by the office when Dad needed her to drop something off for him, and Elmer was smiling every time I saw him. And it was the kind of smile that just made you feel good, like he meant it. Like you were safe in his presence. It was really nice and something I definitely wasn't used to.

A few more people had filtered into the room now. I didn't recognize any of them, but they all wanted to talk to Nate and me. So far, there were no other kids there, just us. I wanted to relax and have fun, but there was something in the back of my mind that just wouldn't let up. I was too worried about my mom to really focus on anything else. I mean, why did Mom have to stay home? It was obvious to me before we even walked in that a lot of people brought their spouses, so why wasn't my mom here too? It just didn't sit well with me, and as hard as I was trying, I just couldn't shake the feeling that something was wrong.

"You're awfully quiet, young lady!" Elmer belted from across the room in his big jolly voice. "I know, this motley crew leaves me speechless most of the time too, I don't blame you! You're a smart one, Jena, just taking it all in first." By now he'd rolled his chair across the room to where I was standing and patted me on the back and said, "Why don't you go find your brother? I bet he's already climbing the lumber stacks!" And with that, I forced a smile, nodded, and looked to my dad to make sure it was okay. He nodded, so I went outside to find Nate. And he, of course, had already climbed to the highest stack of lumber in the yard.

As I started to climb up, he said, "No! You go climb on another stack. I'm on this one!" Great, that's all I needed today, my brother wanting nothing to do with me. Why was I even here? I wished I was at home with Mom. I didn't know how I was going to make it through the day not knowing if she was okay. I found a stack of lumber in the furthest corner of the yard and climbed it and just sat there. I wanted to cry, but the tears wouldn't come. I was just too afraid and uneasy to really function. I tried to focus on the warm feeling of the sun beaming down on my body. I lay down on the stack of wood, closed my eyes, folded my hands over my belly, and started talking to God as I had countless times before.

God, I don't know why my mom can't be here, but please, please look after her at home and keep her safe. Please. And as the tears began to stream down the sides of my face, I just kept praying.

Just as I was just starting to feel a glimmer of peace, I heard, "Jena! Jena! Where are you? Let's go!" My dad was yelling for me to come inside. And just like that, the anxiety flooded back in. It must be hard for people to understand the level of anxiety I always felt. But the abuse was so constant, so extreme, and my dad said unthinkable things during his tirades. I must have heard him tell my mom he'd kill her a thousand times. And I believed it. We all did. I just always knew that one day my Mom, Nate, or I were going to end up dead. I lived every single day in fear of that.

As I rounded the corner of the last wood stack, I could see my dad standing outside his office, holding his hands up in frustration.

"Where in the hell have you been, I've been calling you for five minutes now! Get your ass in here. Let's go. It's time to eat." As he held the door open for me, I ducked swiftly past him so he couldn't slap me in the back of the head or kick me in the butt like he often did when he was annoyed. I made it, though I did feel a wave of wind behind my head. He had swung but missed. I ran up to where Nate was standing a little farther down the hallway and waited for my dad to catch up. My dad went ahead of us while Nate and I intentionally lagged several steps behind him; it always felt safer to put as much distance between us and him as possible. As Dad got about midway down this never-ending hall, a door opened, and a tall, slender woman with long brown hair stepped out into the hall beside my dad.

And in a half of a blink of an eye, my whole world came crashing down on me. "Hey, baby!" she excitedly exclaimed as she reached for my dad's hand and leaned in and kissed him. And as if it was the most natural thing in the world, my dad took her by the hand, and they walked together in front of Nate and me, laughing and enjoying each other. I had never seen my dad be that affectionate to my mom. Ever. My brain literally could not process what was happening right in front of me. My mind was racing and my heart pounding and my stomach twisting. I didn't know what to do, but I knew in that instant that my heart would never be the same. It was crushed. Just destroyed. Of all of the heinous acts my father had committed against us over the years, this is the thing that slayed me. Mind. Heart. And spirit. I was completely broken.

I couldn't even look over at Nate. I would have started weeping out loud if I had seen the hurt in his face. So I just stared straight ahead. But not at them. Past them. Beyond them to some blank space. I wasn't even there anymore. Just gone in every way a person could be gone; I was vacant. And I was numb. I think that was God's way of keeping me safe in that moment because it was in my nature to just scream, "Who the hell are you and why are you touching my dad? Get the hell away from him!" And it wasn't beyond me to ask my dad what the hell he was doing, either. But it just wasn't there. None of it. No words. Barely thoughts. Just lost.

As we entered the picnic area, my dad and this person didn't let go of each other. That was puzzling to me. Did all of these people know? It wasn't a secret? Did these people actually know what my dad was doing to my mom? And they were still laughing and smiling even though my brother and I were standing right here? I didn't get it. What was happening? The next thought that hit me was that these people, who were surely the worst traitors ever to my mom, were about to eat all the food she had so lovingly prepared. Oh, hell no! No. No. No. No. No way! And that woman was definitely not touching my mom's food! So I bolted in front of the two of them and plopped myself down on top of the cooler that was sitting in the center of the picnic area. It was going to take an act of God to make me move.

Within a few seconds, my dad walked over to me and said, "Get up. I need to set the food out. Come on, up." He didn't say it angrily or anything, just matter of fact like. As if he actually thought I was going to comply with this most absurd demand. I just looked up at him. "Come on, get up," he chuckled. I just kept staring at him. "Jena, what are you doing? Get up so I can get the food, now!" And as I began to feel hot tears fill my eyes, I said, "Nope."

"What, Jena?" he asked.

"No, I am not getting up! That woman is not eating my mom's food!" I said much louder, loud enough that she could hear me.

And there it was. The first of many standoffs with my dad. Gone was the girl terrified and always begging and pleading with him. Gone was the girl. Gone forever. "Jena, I am not playing with you, now get your ass up," he said in front of everyone.

"Nope." I had locked it in. He was going to have to physically remove me from the cooler in front of all of these people if he wanted in it. I could see fire in his eyes. And for the first time ever, instead of being afraid of what he was about to do, I was provoking it. I was thinking, let all of these people see who you really are. I mean, obviously they don't care that you're a cheater, but let's see what they think of you when you hit your daughter. Go ahead. Do it. I don't even think I could feel it at this point.

He reached down to pull me up, and I grasped the cooler handles as tightly as I could. The whole cooler began to lift. The tears were still welling but not one had fallen. I stared back at him with fire in my eyes. Fire in my soul. I could feel it. I wasn't moving. And the sooner he realized that, the better off we would all be. Of course, I hadn't thought this through to its inevitable end and what was going to happen when all these people were gone and I was alone with him. No, I was fully committed to standing up for my mom in her absence. And if it cost me my life, well at least I would have left this world saying something that meant something, standing for something. Standing. Not cowering. Not pretending that everything was okay. I could live with that. And I could die with that. But I wasn't moving.

By now, everyone was watching, including this...this...girl that had kissed my dad, who, as I got a better look at her, seemed to be half my dad's age. Disgusting! Elmer had made his way through the crowd at this point and came up and knelt down right beside me. I looked at him, and I could tell in his eyes that he was scared for me and really uneasy. Maybe he knew my dad better than I thought. "Sweetie, do you want to come with me and see all the desserts?" I couldn't speak or I was going to cry, so I just shook my head no. "Are you sure? They have a chocolate cake over there with sprinkles on it that looks really good. Come on, sweetheart." He gently touched my hand. I looked up at him again and that was it, the floodgates opened and the tears just started rolling down my cheeks. I was so embarrassed that all of these people were seeing me cry. And I was angry that they were seeing me cry. Especially that woman. I wanted them to be tears of rage. But they weren't. They were tears of a girl with a fully broken heart, tears of a girl that was never going to be okay again.

As Elmer gently pulled on my hand, I stood up and buried my face in his chest. I felt our feet moving, so I knew we were walking, but I couldn't see where because I was hiding my face in his shirt. It seemed like we walked for a minute or more when I felt him let go, and he kneeled down in front of me and said, "I know it doesn't feel like it right now, but you're going to be okay, Jena. I promise. When God allows our hearts to be broken, he always puts them back together. And do you know what that means, Jena? When God puts something together, it can never be broken again. I know you don't understand what I'm telling you right now and that's okay. But try to believe me. God has you, and he isn't going to let you go. You, your mom, and your brother, you're going to be okay. Okay?"

His voice and his words were just so kind in a moment when I desperately needed someone to be kind to me. Desperately needed someone to see me. See the world of hurt I was carrying. And though our conversation ended there, I think he did know. I think he saw me. And he saw my dad. And he saw it clearly. And just for a minute, there was comfort in that. Realizing that someone else knew. And that someone also knew God and must talk to him an awful lot too because he knew things about God I didn't yet know. But I believed him and could tell that he genuinely cared. I took an unintentional deep breath like you do when you've been crying uncontrollably, and Elmer hugged me one more time. Then he said, "How about you come eat with me today, would you like that?" I still couldn't get any words out, but I nodded yes, and we headed back in to the picnic. My dad never once came over to see how I was or to speak to me. He couldn't have cared less how I was or how I felt. I was sure he was seething about the cooler incident and had no doubt that I'd pay for that later on. I didn't even care. Maybe that was the gift that would come out of the worst moment of my life; that fear finally gave way to anger. And while it didn't feel very good either, it was much better than fear. I didn't feel as powerless. He'd done the worst thing to me that he could ever do—betray my mom. What was left to fear?

I tried to eat, but I couldn't. And I wouldn't even let myself look over at my mom's food because I didn't think I could control my temper if I saw her eating it. So I slipped back out to the lumberyard and climbed back up on the same stack of wood as before. I began to talk to God again. *I don't have any words right now, but if you could just be here with me, that would be good. Please just be here with me and help me however I need help because I know that I do. And God, I hope what Elmer said is true. That you will put me back together so no one can ever break me again.* With that, I closed my eyes and drifted off to sleep.

When I woke, I didn't remember right away where I was, but as I came round, I felt the hard wood beneath me and remembered. I panicked because I didn't know how long I'd been asleep and whether the picnic was still going on. Maybe my dad had left me here. That wouldn't have surprised me. While I was coming out of my sleep fog, I listened for voices but didn't hear any. Then I looked around the parking lot and saw a bunch of cars still there. Okay, so the picnic was still going on. Apparently, my dad had not come looking for me. I wasn't sure if it was just that he didn't care or if he was afraid of what I would say in front of everyone. I knew he wasn't afraid of me one-on-one because he had all the power. But add a roomful of people to the equation and he no longer had the upper hand. And he now knew that I would risk the consequences, that I would take a stand against him publicly. I was sure he was not having any of that. And deep down I knew how dangerous my newfound courage was going to be for me.

But I didn't know the lengths he would go to force me back into submission, to force my silence and my obedience. Up until I saw him kiss that woman, I just thought my dad was an out-of-control, cruel alcoholic and that if he could stop drinking, he would realize all the horrible things he had done to us and he'd be so sorry because he really loved us. I thought his drinking made him a monster. But I was wrong. He just was a monster. And drinking allowed him the freedom to enact his cruelty upon us without conscience. My dad didn't love us. And it was that realization coupled with seeing him betraying my mother in such a deplorable manner that wrecked me completely. And I remember so clearly what I said to God before I climbed down from the lumber stack to go see what was going on, *God, I am never ever going to let anyone treat me the way my dad treats my mom. Never. No matter what. I am never going to need anyone.* I felt good about that resolution. Like I had finally figured it all out. Like I had something to look forward to if I survived my dad. I could look forward to fully controlling my own life and never allowing anyone to hurt me, ever again. The key thing, I decided, was to never need anyone for anything. I was so satisfied with that notion. That might have been the closest thing to contentment that I had ever felt. I couldn't have known then the power those repetitive thoughts would have over me and my future. You tell yourself any one thing for long enough and it becomes your truth. The one you live out of. Even if it's all wrong.

But I had to survive my dad before I could grow up to not need anyone for anything, and that was doubtful. As I walked into the picnic area and spotted my dad, who was glaring in my direction, I wasn't at all sure I'd survive the day. I was beginning to dread the ride home when I remembered about my mom. Was she okay? Did he have someone do something to her while we were gone? I needed to know. Because my initial suspicion that something was terribly wrong made even more sense now that I knew he had a girlfriend. *God, I need to get home! Please protect my mom!*

I could see the picnic was winding down as people began repacking their coolers and saying their good-byes. I realized I hadn't seen Nate since my cooler defiance. I panned around the room but didn't spot him. I hoped he was okay. I knew he was hurting as much as I was. I ran back down the hallway and back out into the lumberyard and started yelling his name. He wasn't answering me. I kind of understood that. I never felt like being found when I was hiding either. So I climbed to the top of the tallest stack of lumber I could find and looked around the yard. I spotted him three stacks over. He was lying on his stomach with his head resting on his hands. I made my way over to him as fast as I could. "Hey, are you okay?" I asked. He didn't respond. I began to rub his back. I knew he couldn't talk. I wasn't ready to talk about it either. So I sat there rubbing his back until I heard our dad calling for us. "Kids, let's go, come on!" My brother popped right up. He was always far more compliant with Dad than I ever was. I like to say he was the smart one. And while we survived the war we were born into differently, we both have the deepest of battle scars that we live out of to this day.

I was the last one to arrive outside my dad's office, and he was standing there staring right through me. Black eyes. I recognized that look. My stomach began to churn but not as intensely as it usually did. I actually believed I was ready to face him, to take him on. What a naïve notion. As we climbed into the car, I sat in the back as usual, but I slid all the way over behind my dad's seat, thinking it would be harder for him to do anything to me because he couldn't see me clearly. That was a pretty dumb move. Because even though he couldn't see me, it put me within reach of his long monkey-like arms.

As my dad began to back out of the yard, he looked over his shoulder in my direction, and I looked down at the floor. That, too, was a dumb move. Before I could even think, my face buckled and my head hit the car window. He had just slapped me so hard I couldn't feel my teeth for a minute. And by the time I'd gathered myself, he was looking straight ahead as if nothing had happened. No words were spoken for what seemed like forever. But I could see the imprint of his hand on my face in his rearview mirror. And I also caught a glimpse of his smirk while I was checking out my face.

The silence was broken when we turned onto our road. "Now listen, you two," he dictated, "you will not ever mention to your mom what you saw today. Do you understand me?" Neither of us responded. I mean how do you respond to that? "Do you two understand me? Because I would hate to think what would happen if you told your Mom. She would be hurt." My brother and I both knew that he wasn't talking about hurt feelings. He was letting us know that if we told Mom about that woman, he would hurt her. I hadn't even thought yet about telling her. She deserved to know, but it would hurt her so much. And she already had so much pain. And my dad still wouldn't let her leave him. So if she knew, he might just kill her. I decided on the spot I'd never tell her what I had seen that day. But what an enormous burden it was carrying that around. Ultimately, I made the choice that I thought would keep her the safest. It wasn't about protecting him; it was about protecting her.

As we pulled into the driveway, I caught another glimpse of my dad looking at me in the rearview mirror, and I thought, *I hate you. I really hate you.* I'd thought it before, but I'd never really felt it was true. Looking back, that seems odd. But I had loved my dad up until that day. I really had. I didn't like him. I didn't trust him. I didn't respect him. I couldn't stand him. But I'd loved him. And until that day, I really believed that deep down, buried under all that dysfunction and rage, he loved us too. Not anymore.

That one day shaped so many things in my life. It was easily the most consequential day of my young life, without a doubt. My fear had given way to anger. I'd declared I'd never need another human being in my entire life. I'd realized I hated my dad. Things were at their lowest, and yet I somehow felt like I had some control over my life for the very first time. I liked it. It was far superior in every way to constantly being scared to death, constantly wanting and waiting on someone, anyone, to take care of and protect me. And far better than loving the father who clearly didn't love me back. It felt like progress. It really did.

Chapter 5

I Won't Tell

The night of the picnic was surprisingly uneventful at home. My dad didn't leave me alone with my mom, though, which was unusual. I could tell he wasn't convinced that his threats and backhand had really gotten through to me. And I did think about what happened that day. I thought about it all night and pretty much every day after. So the next morning when I awoke to my dad standing over my bed telling me to get up, I was definitely rattled. Had I slept through my worst fear? Where was my mom? Why was he in my room? I mean, waking up scared was par for the course for me—I'd never awakened any other way that I could remember—but this was off-the-charts scared. My door had definitely been locked. And I hadn't even heard him come in.

He was half grinning, half glaring, kind of like what you'd imagine the devil looks like.

"Get up, sunshine, we're going to the farm!" he said.

"Where's Mom?" I asked, half awake.

"She's in the kitchen making breakfast, where the hell do you think she is?"

Real nice, Dad, I thought, always so nice. "Okay, I'll get up."

"Yes, you will. Be ready to leave in twenty minutes."

"Is Nate going?" I asked.

"No, it's just you and me today." And with that, he turned and headed down the hallway. The churning in my stomach went from zero to one hundred in a matter of seconds. Why did I have to go by myself? Instinctively, I knew this was somehow tied to what had happened at the picnic and the fact that he wasn't at all satisfied I was going to keep my mouth shut. *Okay, Jena, try not to freak out*, I told myself, *maybe he just doesn't want to leave you alone with Mom until he sufficiently threatens you into silence. Maybe that's all it is, that he's going to talk to you about it again. Talk, meaning he'll tell me that if I open my mouth there will be hell to pay.*

Even though I obviously wasn't conveying to him that I didn't intend to tell my mom, I had already decided on my own not to tell her because that was the safest thing for her. I knew for certain that my dad would never let my mom walk out the door, and never with his kids. And not because he loved us, but because we were his, like property, and he didn't lose his property. No, there was only one way to leave my dad, and that was by ambulance, in a body bag. I guess my open defiance at the picnic really threw him for a loop and now he was seeing me more as a loose cannon than a kid cowering in submission. Well, at least he got that part right. I was done bowing down to him.

But in this case, when I was about to be completely on my own with this monster I called Dad, and at a most isolated location, my

Uncle Harry's farm, I wasn't sure how to formulate a plan of safety. And it hadn't gone over my head that my mom had no idea she should be on high alert for my safety because she had no idea what had happened yesterday. As I made my way into the kitchen, still in my pajamas, I could smell the aroma of bacon cooking before I saw my mom standing over the stove. While it smelled good, my stomach was so tied up that I couldn't even think of eating.

I hugged my mom tightly, and she returned the embrace.

"Love you, Mom."

"I love you too, Jena."

"I have to go get dressed now. Dad said I have to go to the farm with him." I said it almost questioningly but she didn't pick up on it.

"I know, honey, it'll be fine. You like riding on the tractor."

Normally that was true; I did like to ride on the tractors while my dad was picking the cornfields or on the smaller John Deere, but not today. Nooooo. Today I was thinking he might push me off the tractor and I'd fall under those ginormous wheels that were far taller than I was.

I reluctantly headed back down the hall to my room and put on a pair of jeans and a T-shirt. Even though it was pretty hot outside, the mosquitos ate me alive whenever I was there, especially around the pond. As I was getting dressed, I caught a glimpse of myself in the dresser mirror and realized my long brown hair was all knotted up. As I brushed it out, I had a fleeting thought of putting my hair in ponytails. But putting my hair in ponytails at this age was ridiculous and had become a form of pure manipulation on my part and something that I was disgusted by. The thought that he would look at me so adoringly and say, "Now, there's my girl!" if he saw me with ponytails just made me want to puke. I was only his girl when I looked really pretty, had my hair in ponytails, or was winning something that he could brag about and take credit for. It had nothing to do with me. But I had to admit I was still putting my hair in ponytails fairly often to try to put him in, or keep him in, a good mood. My dad just had this thing about wanting my hair in ponytails all the time. He had insisted on it when I was younger. In fact, in almost every family photo, my hair is in ponytails. After a few minutes of blankly staring in the mirror, I sat the brush back down alongside the ponytail holders and turned to make my bed. No ponytails today.

God, I don't know what he has planned for me, but I don't think it's good. Please don't let him hurt me. Please protect me. If you could somehow make him change his mind about taking me that would really be great. Please, God. I don't want to go. I'm scared. I'm really scared. And I know I should put my hair up in these dumb ponytails, but I just can't do it. I don't know why. But really, can ponytails save me from whatever he has in store for me today? Probably not. But you can, God. You are my only hope. I'm not sorry for standing up for my mom yesterday at the picnic. I know that was the right thing to do no matter what he does to me. I would do the same thing today if it happened all over again. I mean, God, you see how he treats her! You see how helpless she is and how good of a person she is, and he's horrible. He's the worst person alive. And then to see him humiliating her behind her back and so publicly. God, it is just more than I can hold inside myself. I feel like I need to reach in and pull it out, but I can't. I can't unsee that. I can't not know that it happened. But you can make me forget it. You parted the Red Sea, surely you can make me forget my dad is cheating on my mom. Please just strike it from my memory, God.

I took a deep breath and let it out and made my way outside, where my dad was loading stuff into his truck. It was one of those old farm-use Ford pickup trucks, blue with a bench seat. Usually I'd have to sit in the middle right beside my dad while my brother or my mom would sit on the other side by the door. But today, since it was just us, I could sit further away from him, which seemed like a really good idea right now. He didn't even acknowledge that I was out there; he just kept loading the truck. I climbed up into the seat and closed the door. I could still smell the remnants of my dad's cigar. He never smoked cigarettes but almost always smoked a cigar when he was driving to the farm. I liked the smell of it. I felt the truck shake as he slammed the tailgate closed, and my stomach did a flip. He climbed in without even looking at me, and as we backed out of the driveway, I couldn't help but fear my fate. I knew one thing for certain—he was not in a good mood, and he wasn't interested in mincing words with me. And because I'd studied him more than any schoolbook, I knew this was not good. Not at all.

Ten minutes passed, fifteen, and still not one word. I could feel the sun coming through the window dance on the side of my cheek, and it made me want to close my eyes and lean into it, but I knew better. Sure as anything, he'd see my eyes closed and think I might actually be relaxing and—*wham!*—he'd hit me upside the head to remind me that there was no relaxing in his presence. It was like he saw it as a sign of disrespect if you didn't outwardly demonstrate your fear of him. And in our family, I was the only stubborn mule. It wasn't like I really planned to buck his system. I tried to talk myself into falling in line most of the time for everyone else's sake, but I just couldn't cower to him all the time, even if it meant paying the consequences. And it usually did. But what my dad had learned about me was that the surest way to get me to submit was to make me fear him harming my mom. That worked like magic every time. But if it was just my hide on the line, more often than not I would find a way, even if it was subtle, to take a stand against his tyrannical rule, especially now that I had gotten older.

As we came up on the old general store just a few miles away from Uncle Harry's farm, I wondered if he'd stop like he always did to get beer and sodas. Every time we stopped there, he'd let me and Nate fill up a little brown bag of candy. I was thinking today wouldn't be a candy day, and I didn't think I could eat it anyway. He pulled into the little gravel parking lot, and as he shifted the truck into park, he said, "Let's go."

I got out and followed him into the store, not even looking in the direction of the candy aisle. Suddenly I was jolted by a loud familiar voice. "How you doin'!" big Erney yelled at me, even though he was standing right beside me. Big Erney was a staple at the general store. He was probably in his twenties, but mentally he was more like a five-year-old. He was a big, burly country boy who always wore the same blue jeans and flannel shirt. I knew he was handicapped, but I wasn't sure how or why. But I loved seeing Erney with his over-the-top joyful spirit and larger-than-life smile. He just made me smile.

"Hi, Erney, how are you?" I said.

"Good. Good. Good. How you doin'!" he said with that infectious smile of his.

I think that is all I've ever heard him say. *How you doin'!* And he didn't ask it like a question, it was more of a statement. I'm not sure he knew what he was saying, but he sure loved saying it. My dad spoke to him and, as always, was nice to Erney. That was a puzzling thing about my dad. He was the nicest person you ever wanted to see when talking to someone like Erney or a person clearly down on their luck. And he was quick to offer help or money or a ride. I'd never seen him pass up a person like that even one time. And while those moments made me feel really good about my dad, like there was something redeemable about him, I always wondered why he didn't treat us that way. I just never understood that. I mean, he didn't even know them, but he would bend over backward to help them. I sure wished I were Erney today. I'd have given anything not to have an understanding of my own situation or to be someone that my dad would be nice to. My dad finished paying for his case of Budweiser and headed out the old wooden door, which snapped closed on its own. I didn't make the door before it closed, and I'm pretty sure that was intentional on my dad's part. Any other time, he would have held the door and let me go out first.

As he situated his beer in the cooler full of ice in the back of the truck, I got in my seat and started talking to God again.

Well, God, we're really close to the farm now. I can tell that he is furious with me. I don't know why he couldn't have just talked to me like a normal person on the way over here and asked me not to tell Mom. That would give me the chance to tell him I was never going to tell her. What am I even saying, God? What has ever been normal in my whole life? What is normal? Maybe everybody lives like this. Is that possible? No. Other kids just seem too happy. Like they don't have a care in the world. Nate and I always seem distant and like we are preoccupied. So I'd say, no, most people probably don't live like we do. But I don't know how they live, God. I have no idea. And I guess knowing that isn't going to help me right now anyway. But, God, you can help me. So please, please help me. At least make him say something so I know where I stand. The waiting is killing me. What am I waiting for? What is going to happen when we get there? Are we just picking corn? God, please let us pick corn on the tractor that is closed in and air-conditioned so I don't have to worry about him pushing me off the open tractor. If I go under those wheels, that's it for me.

My uncle's farm was enormous, more than one hundred acres, I think. We pulled up to the locked gate, and my dad unlocked the padlock and chain and opened the gate. Once he'd pulled through, he closed it back up and locked it, which was odd. He would typically just leave it open until we left because sometimes my uncles and other farmhands showed up to work too. That made me uneasy, but then everything he did made me uneasy, so I tried to force my mind onto other things, like noticing all the butterflies circling this one area of the field. They were bright yellow and so pretty. I was snapped back to reality when my dad took a right toward the pond instead of going straight ahead to the tractor area. Why were we going to the pond? Surely we weren't fishing today. He continued driving past the pond, even though there really weren't any paths or roads cut out beyond the pond. My heart was pounding. I wanted so badly to ask him where we were going, but I was too afraid. So I said nothing. The truck finally stopped, and he said, "Get out." Just matter of fact like. So I got out. The grass here was a little high, and I was terrified of snakes, so I was careful where I stepped.

"Come back here!" he yelled, motioning me to the back of the truck. "Here, carry this!" He handed me an empty white 5-gallon bucket, and I took it by the handle. He reached into the cooler and grabbed a few beers with one hand and picked up a shovel with the other. What did he need a shovel for? My heart started to race. "Follow me," he said. We walked in front of the truck about fifty feet and he stopped. "Sit down," he said, so I sat on the ground with the bucket beside me. He picked up the bucket, turned it upside down, and patted the top of it. "Sit here." I moved to the bucket.

I was fixated on his every move at this point and was seriously contemplating taking off running. He was fast, but if I had a head start, he would never catch me. And if I ran out through the cornfield, he would never find me. I probably couldn't find my own way out, but I'd be safe.

Except from snakes, I guess. But right now I'd be willing to take my chances. He stared at me for a minute, and I held his stare. Not out of defiance this time but out of concern. If he swung that shovel at me, I wanted to be prepared. He walked about twenty feet to the left of me, popped the top on his Budweiser, and downed it in a matter of seconds. He crushed the can in his hands, tossed it to the side, and started digging into the ground with the shovel. What was he digging a hole for? The answer hit me before I could even finish the question in my head. Oh my God, was he going to kill me and bury me out here? Was he digging that hole for me?

Oh, God, no. God, no! God, please help me! Please, you have to see me right now! I can't wait! You have to help me. Tell me what to do. Do I run? Now? Please, God, what do I do?! Oh, God, please stop him!"

I didn't want to reveal the panic in my face, didn't want him to be onto what I thought he was doing. So I made myself start playing with the overgrown grass blades around me. And I did my best to act like I wasn't about to pass out from sheer fear. But I felt like I might. My mind raced and I tried so hard to slow all the jumbled thoughts that were flooding my brain. I surveyed my surroundings to see how far away the start of the cornfield was. I thought I could get there before he caught me. Especially if he had no idea I was about to make a run for it. But what if he hit me in the head with the shovel before I could get there? Then it could go really bad really fast. The keys were still in the ignition of the truck, maybe I could get in it and drive away. But I wasn't really sure how to drive. I mean I had driven on the farm before, but I wasn't sure I could get backed out of here without running into a ditch or the pond or something. What should I do? I didn't know. I didn't know what to do!

God! Please help me! I need your help right now! Please, God! Right now! Before it's too late! If you don't help me, God, he's going to kill me!"

My dad just kept digging. He was making pretty good time digging this hole in between drinking beers. I needed to make a decision about what I was going to do.

God, I know you can see me. And I know you can see my dad. You see what he's doing. And only you know if he's going to kill me or not. I am so scared, God, and I want to scream and cry out loud, but no one would even hear me. God, please, if I'm not going to make it out of this, just grant me these two things. Please. I will never ask you for anything else until I see you. Please help me because I need you so badly right now just like the night I climbed into my closet years ago. Please, God, just two things. Please don't let it hurt. And please take my fear away. I don't want to die so afraid.

And that's all I could get out before the tears started to pour down my face. The grave reality of my situation was setting in, and I was so frightened...of everything. But I didn't want my dad to see or hear me cry, so I turned around on the bucket facing the other way. I could not stop the tears from falling, and I couldn't ease the heaviness of my heart or the sheer terror I was feeling

As the tears continued flowing, I felt something on my hand. I went to jerk it away, thinking it was a mosquito, but it wasn't, it was one of those tiny yellow butterflies. And it landed right on my hand. For some reason this made me cry harder. How I wished I were that butterfly so I could just fly away.

Jona, get it together, I thought to myself. *You have to stop crying or he is going to hear you. He probably already has.* Slowly I got the tears to cease, and I dried my face with my hands and tried to focus on all the little living creatures I saw in the grass. I saw ants scurrying about on the ground going in and out of the same hole. I saw a ladybug climbing a blade of grass. And I still saw the little butterfly sitting on a wildflower poking up from the grass. Its wings were fluttering and I kept watching it, wondering what it was thinking. Did it think? Did it feel? It was so little, and its wings looked so fragile, like they could break so easily. But it seemed really happy sitting on that flower. Content.

At this point, I think my mind had reconciled with my heart that

I might not be leaving this farm today. And as crazy as it sounds, I wasn't terrified like I had been a half an hour earlier. Maybe I was just ready to go. I started thinking about heaven like I did so often. I could picture how bright the sun would be there, how warm it would feel. And I imagined God's warm embrace and felt a calm come over me. I thought about all the bright colors of the flowers in heaven and about the butterflies. I bet there would be fields and fields of butterflies. And I'd never hurt again. I would never feel pain again. I would never be scared again. Maybe God had to let this happen to me so my mom and my brother could be rescued. And the more I thought about that, the calmer I felt inside.

Okay, God. Okay…

I swiveled back around on my bucket, and I was shocked to see how deep the hole already was. I didn't want to look at it, so I just looked down. But the calm didn't fade.

God, you heard me. And you answered me. The two things I asked for… please don't let it hurt. And please take my fear. Tears welled up, but they weren't tears of anguish, they were tears of gratitude. I was so grateful that even though God might not let me leave this farm, he'd taken away my fear. And I believed with all of my heart that he wouldn't let it hurt either. There was no other explanation on planet Earth for why I wasn't still scared to death than God had answered my prayer! God had done something for me beyond what I could ever have done for myself. I was rarely able to fend off fear. But God is not limited like I am. And he is more powerful than my dad. And I was going to be home soon. My real home. A forever home. And I would never be afraid again. And I would never be hurt again.

"I will never leave you nor forsake you." That verse just kept playing over and over again in my mind.

And then I heard a *clang!* and "Jena, come over here!" Without conscious thought, I stood and walked over to my dad. I wouldn't look into the hole, but I could somehow sense how deep it was. I just kept looking at my dad. When I got within a few feet of him and the hole he'd dug, he said, "Jena, lay down here." So I sat down and I let my feet dangle into the hole, still trying my best to avoid looking into it. I started to turn my body around to climb down, and he said abruptly, "What are you doing, Jena! Just lay down right here," he motioned with his hands, "beside the hole, so I can see how long it is." So I lay down alongside the hole. "Yep, that'll just about do it! Okay, hop up." I stood up. "Brush yourself off, Jena, you have dirt all over your back!"

I was so confused. Why did I need to wipe myself off if I was going in that hole? But I didn't question him; I just did as he told me. He walked over to the bucket, picked it up, and started walking toward the truck, and I just stood there, not sure what to do. He realized I wasn't behind him and said, "Jena, come on, let's go!" as if he was miffed that I didn't know to follow him. He tossed the shovel and bucket into the back of the truck, grabbed another beer from the cooler, popped the top, and climbed into the truck. I still wasn't sure what was happening, but I hadn't said one word since we left the house, and I didn't feel any words in my mouth now either. My dad circled around the pond and headed back toward the path we'd come in on. Instead of taking a right to go to the tractor, he took a left to head out of the farm. I really didn't know what to think, but I felt an enormous sense of relief and that same peaceful feeling I'd had back at the hole. I wasn't worried. I wasn't scared. I just wondered what was happening. And what the hole was for.

We got a few miles down the road and he said, "Jena, you're taller than your mom now, aren't you?" I nodded yes. "I can't hear you, are you taller than your mom?"

"Yes," I muttered. My voice cracked because I hadn't used it yet and I'd been crying. I cleared my throat and said it again. "Yes. I'm taller than Mom, why?"

"I thought so. That's why I wanted to measure you against the hole back there."

Immediately, I put together what he was saying, and before I could gather a single thought, I blurted out, "Dad, I am never going to tell Mom you have a girlfriend! Never! I am never going to tell anyone!"

"I know, Jena. I just wanted to make sure you understood me." And with that he looked right at me and said, "Do you? Do you understand me, Jena?"

I held his stare. "Yes."

"Yes, what?"

"Yes, I understand."

"Yes, what!" he said again.

"Yes sir, I understand."

And with that, he looked back at the road and didn't say another word to me the whole ride home.

And I did understand. I understood it wasn't me he was going to put in that hole. And maybe no one was ever going in that hole. But I knew one thing for sure, he'd enjoyed making me think it was for me, and now he was enjoying making me think that it was for my mom. And with that sick display, he bought the assurance of my permanent silence about what had happened at the picnic.

But what he couldn't know was that with that evil demonstration of his, that physical display of how far he was willing to go, he'd set into motion things that no one but God could stop. I knew what I had to do. I didn't know how to do it. But I knew I had to kill my dad before he could kill my mom.

I was glad he'd decided on silence for the remainder of the ride home because I needed to think. I forced my mind into sorting through the nightmare that the last two days of my life had been. I hadn't put it all together yet. I mean, why did my dad even take Nate and me to the picnic? If he hadn't taken us, we wouldn't have known he was cheating on Mom, and he wouldn't have had to worry about us telling. There had to be a reason he wanted us to see him with her. Had she asked to meet us? And if so, why? Why would she want to meet us? I didn't get it. But one thing I knew for sure—my dad couldn't have cared less how much that hurt Nate and me. Why had he even wanted kids? He didn't love us, he did nothing but hurt us, and he never even considered how we felt about anything. My dad had never once asked me how I was, how I felt, if I was okay. Nothing. He didn't have personal conversations with Nate and me. He just made statements. He talked at us. Never with us. And hell would freeze over before my dad would ever say he was sorry about anything!

I was so thankful when we turned onto our road. I couldn't wait to run in the house and hug my mom. But I knew I needed to be careful of every step I made right now. I shouldn't seem so eager. Mom was going to wonder why we'd only been gone for three hours when usually it was an all-day thing to pick the corn. And how would I look at my mom without bursting out crying? It was so hard to hold so much in. I couldn't process it all. The picnic and my dad's girlfriend. Then making me watch him dig a hole that I thought he was going to bury me in. I wished I had someone I could talk to; someone I could tell. I desperately needed someone to talk to. Someone to really talk to. But I knew that wasn't a thought worth spending any real time on. My mom, Nate, and I, we never told anyone what happened to us. It was like we just knew how that would end for us.

But I did daydream about the police hauling Dad off all the time. Thankfully, I was smart enough to know how that would go in advance. Law enforcement's idea of helping around these parts was to have a chat with the offender and tell him he needed to calm down and behave. And even if they did bother to take him in, he'd be back in a matter of hours. And then there would be some kind of hell to pay. No, we'd learned that we were stuck suffering in silence. His shame was safe with us.

I must have wondered a thousand times how my mom got so unlucky as to marry him of all the men in the world. Talk about opposites. They were night and day. My mom was a country girl, while my dad was very much the city slicker type. And Mom was such a mild-mannered person. She was the nicest, gentlest, most honest person you'd ever meet. She was naturally pretty and never wore any makeup. And she rarely wore anything other than jeans and sneakers. I'd seen my mom in heels maybe five times, and that was on the rare occasions when she and my dad had gone out with his sister Renee and her husband to the dinner theater. My mom was the best person I knew. She was the kind of person that everyone loved instantly. I'd never known a soul that didn't just adore my mom. Well, except my dad. But he didn't love anyone.

Chapter 6

A Close Watch

I spent the next week pretending to be sick so I didn't have to go to school. I was terrified of leaving my mom alone ever since my dad had dug that hole out at the farm. I couldn't eat. I could barely sleep. I knew that he had to go, and I knew that it was going to have to be me that did it, but I had no idea how. The mere thought of it made me want to vomit. And I had thrown up more in the last week than I had in several months combined, probably three or four times a day. Every time I pictured that hole and my mom in it, I had to run to the bathroom. I hadn't had one single moment of rest since the farm incident. My mind had been spinning ever since, and the constant anxiety was at an all-time high. I couldn't shake it. How was I going to kill my own dad? I mean, I'd wished it on him countless times, I'd begged God to kill him for as long as I could remember. But really doing it was completely different. I didn't want to kill him, but I knew I had to or he was going to kill my mom. And if that happened, it would be my fault because I was the only one who knew what he was planning to do. *God, help me, please. I don't know what to do.*

I was pretty sure that my dad knew why I'd been staying home, and it sure did seem like he was gloating over it. Like he was proud of himself for finally being able to scare me into full obedience. Every time I looked at him, it made me sick. I tried to avoid looking at him at all costs. It was also hard to look at him because I knew that I had to kill him, and I didn't want to start feeling bad about that and back out of doing it. I couldn't back out. It was either him or my mom, and I chose my mom. I wondered if he knew what I was thinking? Nah. There was no way he would think that I would have the guts to do something like that. He thought I was too afraid of him now to do anything out of line. He was right. And he was wrong. I was more afraid of what he was capable of than I'd ever been before; which is why I had to act. And soon. When the fear becomes too great, you're forced to act. Either that, or lay down and die and accept whatever fate comes your way. And I wasn't willing to do that because he'd shown me what my fate would be: a life without my mom.

On that Friday, my dad told my mom that I had to go to school next week, no more staying at home. I heard her tell him okay, but she said that if I was still sick, she'd need to take me to the doctor first. He assured her that there was nothing really wrong with me other than wanting to be at home instead of school. He put his foot down and told her it was the end of the conversation. Though I dreaded having to leave my mom, I had known it was only a matter of time and I'd have to go back. But it also made me feel pressure to figure out a way to get rid of my dad before then.

I didn't know what to do because every time I told myself that I had to seriously sit down and formulate a plan, my mind would wander away to something else. Really, how does a kid figure out a way to kill someone? I was scared of my dad's guns, and I didn't know how to use them. If I used a knife and he saw me coming, he'd just take it from me and kill me. I had no idea how to kill my dad. And thinking about it made me sick to my stomach.

Saturday, my dad took my brother and headed to the farm, and I stayed home and helped my mom out in the garden. While I didn't really like pulling weeds, I did like spending time with her. We didn't really talk much, but we'd never really talked all that much, not about anything important. My mom was not a talker; she demonstrated her love in other ways, by hugging me a lot and letting me climb up in her lap in the big velvety rocking chair. She'd let me sit there and rock with her for an hour if I wanted to, even though I was bigger than her. Just being around her and away from my dad was peaceful. And I always loved when she'd say it was lunchtime when we'd been working outside in the heat because she'd make us a big pitcher of sweet iced tea and bologna and cheese sandwiches with chips. It was one of my favorite lunches, and just getting to sit there with her and eat was a joyful time for me. Simple. But joyful. I was so grateful for those rare moments with my mom when we could be together and not be afraid.

Sunday after church, my mom began preparing our usual big family dinner where most of my dad's siblings and their families would come congregate. My mom was the best cook in the world; everyone said so. She made everything from scratch, and it was so good! These big family dinners had pluses and minuses in my mind. On one hand, it was a day that I knew my dad wouldn't be able to hurt my mom or Nate and me because there was an audience. And the great food was always a big plus! On the minus side, my dad usually got pretty drunk at these dinners and at some point would end up outside with everyone, causing an argument with one of his sisters over something stupid. It was always over something stupid. Inevitably, my dad would end up hitting one or more of his sisters. He even choked Aunt Brie at one of these family dinners. One of my uncles had to pull him off of her. When these things happened, I always thought, "Don't they wonder what happens to us when they aren't here?" I mean, if he acted this way with his own siblings, how did they think he treated us? But no one ever said anything. Everyone was too afraid to stand up to my dad. Except maybe Aunt Renee. I'd overheard her telling him that he needed to stop drinking and mistreating everyone before he had no one left to mistreat.

This was the same aunt I had overheard talking to my mom the previous year, asking her if she thought that my dad may be acting inappropriately with me. I was shocked to hear her say something like that, and it really upset me. I knew what she was inferring and was disgusted by it. I know my dad is a bad person, but he's never done anything like that to me. I was offended for my dad. I wanted to burst into the kitchen and give her a piece of my mind, but I decided it was best to just listen around the corner to the rest of what she had to say.

She went on to say that it wasn't normal for a father to take such an interest in his daughter and brag about her all the time. Aunt Renee said it was strange that my dad would brag about my looks and how fast I was, how smart I was. She felt like it crossed a line into something unnatural, that he was too adoring of me. I could tell my mom was taken aback by her suggestion as she stammered to find words to respond.

"Oh, Renee. I don't think so. I...I really don't. Richard just...he just...is really proud of Jena. And I think he sees himself in her, or what he wanted to be. So he pins his hopes on her. That's all it is."

"Well, I'm not so sure that's all it is. I don't like the way he looks at her. I think you should keep a close eye on that, Wendy. A really close eye on that. That kind of damage can't be undone, you know?"

I was so mad at Aunt Renee. It was so disgusting what she was saying, and it put horrible thoughts in my head that took a long time to get out. But I eventually forgave her because, of all of my dad's siblings, she was the kindest to my mom.

She and her husband, Uncle Sam, would invite us over for dinner every few months, and I always looked forward to going. Aunt Renee had a cookie jar full of M&M's, and she would offer them to Nate and me almost as soon as we walked through the door. And Aunt Renee's house always smelled so good and was decorated like royalty lived there; everything was gold trimmed, even her plates! She wasn't nearly as good a cook as my mom, but I loved how she would set her table so fancy and put all of the food in crystal dishes. It was all so beautiful. They lived in the city about an hour and a half away. It was at one of these dinners that my dad would give Aunt Renee and Uncle Sam a much better glimpse of what we were dealing with at home.

Aunt Renee's son, Travis, was in his mid-twenties and looked a bit like a hippie, albeit a very handsome hippie. He had long blond hair and piercing blue eyes and a thick mustache. I thought he was so cool, and he was always really nice to Nate and me. He had joined us for dinner, and as we sat there chatting, I could tell that my dad was getting agitated that he wasn't the center of attention or the one controlling the conversation. The more I sensed this, the quieter I got. My mom too. But Aunt Renee was so proud of Travis, and her eyes danced as he shared his stories with us.

All of a sudden, my dad slammed his fist down on the table and told Travis that everything he was saying was the biggest bunch of bullshit he'd ever heard. We all froze. But Travis chuckled and said, "Well, Richard, I'm sorry you feel that way. But there are children present at the table, so I think it'd be best if you showed a little self-control." My heart fell into my stomach, but before I could process what was happening, my dad had jumped up and ripped the tablecloth from the dining room table, which caused most of the food to land on Aunt Renee's nice carpet. Uncle Sam wrapped his arms around my dad from behind as he lunged for Travis while the rest of us quickly cleared out of the way. My dad wrangled himself free from Uncle Sam's grip and told Travis to wait there, that he had something for him. As my dad stormed out of the house, Aunt Renee frantically tried to get Travis to escape out of a back bedroom window and run. But Travis didn't want to go. He kept saying that he wasn't afraid of my dad, which worried me because I knew that he needed to be.

Uncle Sam insisted that Travis get out of the house immediately, so he finally agreed. He could see how frightened Nate and I were, and he didn't want to make that worse, so he fled through a window. Aunt Renee yelled to my mom to get Nate and me in the back as well, but by then we heard the front door open again, and we knew my Dad was back. My mom pulled Nate and me behind a chair in the living room and had us all kneel down. I could see around the chair, and I saw my dad storm back in with a tire iron in his hands. He waved it around and yelled for Travis to show himself. Aunt Renee and Uncle Sam talked to my dad from across the room and tried anything they could to diffuse him, but he was too drunk and too angry to be reasoned with.

My dad turned the house upside down looking for Travis, and when he couldn't find him, he announced that we were leaving. I was so glad that Travis had gotten away unharmed, but the thought of what could have happened to him if my dad had found him haunted me. My aunt pleaded with my dad to stay the night and sleep it off, but he was having none of that and ordered Mom, Nate, and me to get in the car. Uncle Sam refused to let my dad drive us home and kept getting in my dad's way so he couldn't get in the car. Finally, my dad agreed to let my mom drive. I prayed my aunt could talk him into staying the night so nothing bad would happen to us, but it wasn't to be. Needless to say, we were never invited back to Aunt Renee's house again.

All the way home, I kept my eyes glued to my dad, who was sitting in the front passenger seat. I was afraid he was going to start attacking my mom while she was driving, but halfway home he passed out and began to snore. I could finally breathe. Once home, my mom tried to wake my dad but was unable to, so we went inside and went to bed. I slept on my mom's floor so I could hear if he came in later, but he never did. He slept all night in the car.

The next day we all acted like nothing had happened. I was at the age where this had begun to annoy me tremendously. Why did he get a pass on his crazy behavior all the time? It was hard for me to understand how my mom could shift gears from the abuse and seem genuinely happy or joyful at times. I just didn't get it; there was absolutely nothing about our lives that could be considered joyful. And I was never happy. Neither was Nate. I spent countless hours trying to figure that one out, and all I could come up with was that, while my dad was steeped so heavily in a long family history of alcoholism and abuse, my mom was steeped just as heavily in faith and a happy, stable upbringing. She'd tell Nate and me stories about how she grew up, and it always sounded like a fairy tale to me. I loved hearing her talk about it, and I'd try to imagine what it must have been like. The only time I could really envision it was when we would visit Grandma Beck. I loved going to Grandma Beck's; you could just feel the love when you walked through the front door of her charming country house. She was always so happy to see us, and she would have a pantry and refrigerator stocked full of all kinds of amazing home-cooked foods. I could see why my mom was such a great cook. And there wasn't a bad bone in Grandma Beck's body; she radiated goodness. Just like my mom.

Don't get me wrong, it made me feel really good that my mom didn't seem as affected by the abuse as Nate and I were, but it was hard to understand. Having been born into this dysfunctional way of life, it was all that Nate and I knew. Our foundation was built on fear and shaped by my dad's alcoholism and abuse. We didn't know what joy was because we hadn't experienced it. And we knew nothing of stability or hopefulness. But my mom had enjoyed twenty-five years of a happy, stable life prior to meeting my dad. She knew something better existed because she'd experienced it, and I think that allowed her to have hope.

Sunday dinner wound down, and everyone headed home. I always dreaded when everyone left, especially if my dad was really drunk and had been fighting. It usually spilled over into our night.

Most of my dad's family were alcoholics. His dad was a raging alcoholic who beat his mom throughout their entire marriage until he died. Even through her fourteen years of pregnancy, he still beat her. I don't think I ever heard my Grandma Parks say anything other than "I reckon so," and "I wouldn't know." I think maybe my granddad had beaten the life out of her and she was just a shell of a person without any real thoughts or opinions left of her own. It made me really sad.

I don't remember much about my granddad other than his full head of jet-black hair and his ice-blue eyes. He was already sick with lung cancer at my earliest memory of him, but I could remember going to their house for Sunday dinners when he was still alive, and he'd sit at the end of the table just staring at each of us but never saying a word. When he would speak, it would be to tell Grandma to get him something. He would just bark orders at her. He was a scary man. I'd heard horror stories about him from all my dad's sisters. Strangely enough, I'd never heard my dad or any of his brothers say a bad word about him. They always sang his praises and talked about how hard he worked to put food on the table for their big family. They talked about how strong he was and how physically tough he was. I tended to believe my aunts, especially when I thought about how my dad turned out. He'd had to learn to behave this way somewhere.

But this week we got lucky. My dad was just moderately drunk and didn't seem angry. He poured himself a drink and asked my mom if she wanted one. My mom virtually never drank, so I didn't know why he'd even ask her that. She only drank alcohol maybe once a year on New Year's at the family party my dad threw at our house every year.

"No, thank you. I'm good," she said.

"Ah, come on, Wendy, live a little. One drink won't kill you." He pulled down two glasses from the cabinet. My mom didn't say anything, and I knew that she didn't want to upset the apple cart. She'd drink a drink if she had to in order to keep the peace. We all appeased my dad any way we could.

Dad sent us to get ready for bed and reminded me that I was to be on the bus in the morning to go to school. That thought snapped me back to reality. I was supposed to be trying to figure out how to get rid of my dad.

Chapter 7
Someone Help Me!

I woke to the light streaming through my blinds and hoped against all odds that I could somehow wrangle another day at home. Glancing at my alarm clock, I saw I still had twenty minutes before I had to get up, but I decided to get moving. Though I rarely ate breakfast because I was always too nervous first thing in the morning, today I was feeling particularly hungry. I headed down the hall toward the kitchen, and Nate was already sitting there eating cereal. Mom wasn't in there, which was unusual.

I headed back down the hall to find Mom, and as I stepped into her bedroom, I noticed she was still in bed. Mom was never still in bed, she was always the first one up fixing my dad a cooked breakfast and his nasty raw egg drink.

"Mom," I whispered. No answer.

I walked around to her side of the bed and saw that her face didn't look right. Not beaten up, just not like Mom. "Mom." I rubbed her shoulder. Nothing. My heart sank. I put my ear right up to her mouth to see if she was breathing. I couldn't tell, so I laid my hand on her stomach and felt it move. Oh, thank God! But something still wasn't right. I couldn't wake her. She was mumbling but not talking. Something was definitely wrong.

I screamed, "Someone help me! Help me! Now! Something is wrong with Mom!"

"Mom! Mom! Can you hear me? Talk to me, please! What is wrong?" I was frantic.

There was no phone in my parents' room, and I was scared to leave her alone, but I had to get help. I ran out to the kitchen, and no one was in there, so I ran out to the garage. My dad was putting some of his tools away.

"Dad! Something is wrong with Mom! You have to come, hurry! Something is wrong!" I was yelling at the top of my lungs.

"What are you talking about, Jena? Your mom is sleeping. She's just tired. Let her sleep." He couldn't have seemed less concerned.

"Dad, no! I'm telling you, I was just in there, something is wrong! She can't speak. Something is wrong! I'm calling 911!"

"Jena! Settle down. Your mom is fine. Let's go look."

"Hurry, Dad! Hurry up!"

I ran through the house as fast as I could to get to Mom, and she was still the same. My dad made his way over to her, knelt down, and felt her head.

"Wendy, honey. Are you okay? Jena is worried about you."

My mom mumbled something inaudible and groaned.

"See, Dad?" I started sobbing. "Something is really wrong! Call 911! Call them!"

"Jena!" my dad said sternly, "Calm down! You're not helping

the situation with your hysterics!"

"Dad, something is really wrong with Mom! You can see that! Why aren't you worried? I'm calling 911!" And as I turned to race down the hall, my dad grabbed me in a bear hug from behind and told me to calm down.

"All this yelling isn't helping your mom. She probably has the flu. I'll tell you what. I'll call Aunt Linda and have her come right over and take your mom to the doctor, okay?"

"No, Dad! Let me go! That's not quick enough. She lives a half hour away! Mom needs help now! Right now! You need to take her to the hospital! We need to go now!" I screamed as I fought to get out of his grasp.

"Jena, I'm telling you what we're going to do. Now you need to listen to me. I want you to climb in bed with your mom and make sure she's okay while I go call Linda! She'll be here right away, and I have to go to work." He loosened his grip on me, and part of me wanted to race down the hall and call 911, but I didn't. I don't know why I didn't. He called Linda and told her that my mom was sick and might need to go to the doctor and asked her to please come over right away. He told her he had to go to work but that I was with her.

I couldn't believe my dad wasn't more worried. A blind person could see something was wrong with Mom. And how could he even think of going to work when my mom was lying there suffering? What was wrong with him? He wasn't even human. As cruel as he'd been to us our whole lives, I still couldn't believe he was actually going to leave and not help my mom. My mind was spinning, and my heart was racing, and I'd never been so panicked in my life.

My dad told me that he would call later to check on Mom and that I should go get in bed with mom and hug her because that would make her feel better.

I cried as he turned to walk out the door. I can't even describe the pain I felt that he wasn't going to help my mom. He was so cold, so indifferent. And I felt so helpless. As the door closed behind him, I raced back down the hall to Mom.

She still looked the same, but she was still breathing. "Mom, I'm right here. I'm right here with you. Linda is coming, and we're going to get you to the hospital. Mom? Should I call 911? Mom, I don't know what's wrong, I think I should call 911."

My hesitancy to call 911 was evidence of the years of abuse I'd sustained all my life. You're under the full control of your abuser and so afraid to act on your own, so afraid of the consequences. Here my mom lay in her bed, really ill, something really wrong, and every single fiber of my being was telling me to call 911, and yet because my dad insisted that I didn't, I didn't move to make that call. I anguish over that still.

I ran a washcloth under cold water and laid it on her forehead. I kissed her cheek gently and placed my hand on her stomach to make sure she was breathing. She was.

"W...aat..." My Mom was trying to tell me something, but I couldn't make it out.

"Mom, what? Please say it again. Please, Mom."

She just groaned. My heart was pounding out of my chest. *God, please, please pleeeeeeeaaasse, God! You have to help me. I'm not asking. I'm telling you. You have to help us! Please! Save my mom! Please, God! If you take her, I'm coming with her! I promise you that! God, please, I'm begging you. I'm begging you! Heal my Mom. Please! Tell me what to do! How do I help her! God, do I call 911? Please, God, I'm all alone here, and I don't know what to do! You have to help me! God, don't take her. Please don't take her. Help me!* I pleaded as I cried and cried and cried. My whole body heaved. I had never felt more lost, alone, or terrified. And I wasn't going to take no from God on this one. Not on this one. I meant every word I said. If he took her, I was coming too.

My mom tried to tell me something, but I could not understand her at all. It wasn't whole words, just sounds or beginnings of words.

I ran down the hall to get her some water, thinking that if she could sip some water maybe that would help. And it would definitely encourage me that she would be okay. I raced back into her room with the water and kneeled right in front of her.

"Mom, can you try to sip this water? Mom, can you? Can you hear me?"

She tried to reach for my hand but couldn't. And I was afraid to move her. Afraid to try to sit her up. I didn't want to hurt her, and I didn't know what was wrong. So I put my hand under her head and lifted it as gently as I could and brought the water glass to her. I was able to get a little bit in her mouth, but most of it dribbled down her chin. But she swallowed a little bit. I saw it. I didn't know if that was good, but it felt hopeful to me. Or at least I wanted it to be a good sign.

Finally, I heard the gravel in the driveway and heard a car door slam. "Jena! Jena! Where is your mom? Jena!" Linda yelled through the house.

"Here! We are back here! In Mom's room!"

Linda rounded the corner and gasped when she saw Mom. "Jena, tell me what happened! Tell me! Did your dad do this?"

"I don't know. I just found her this way this morning. I wanted to call 911, but Dad wouldn't let me, and then he just left. Please, please, help my mom!" I cried.

"It's okay, Jena, calm down. I'm here and we're going to help your Mom. Wendy? Sweetie? Can you hear me? Can you talk to me? I need to get you up and in the car. We need to get you to the doctor. Can you tell me what hurts? Wendy?"

My mom just groaned; she really could not respond.

"Jena, I want you to help me get your mom up, okay? Gently. And we're going to move her out to my car and get her to the hospital."

"Can't we just call 911? Please! I think we should call them!"

"Jena, honey, try to listen to me, okay? I know you're scared. I'm scared too, but I'm here now and we're going to help your mom. I can get her to the hospital quicker than an ambulance can get here. If we call them, we'd have to wait at least twenty minutes for them to get out here. You live in the middle of nowhere, Jena. We have to move quickly. Okay?"

I hadn't thought of it that way, but Aunt Linda was right, it would take too long for them to get out here, and we could be at the hospital by then.

"Okay. Tell me what to do," I said.

"Get on that side of your mom, and I will lift her from this side.

We're going to get our shoulders up under hers on each side and gently walk her out to my car. Okay? Ready, lift."

My mom was so small, it was easy to lift her up. But as we moved her, she groaned louder.

"We're hurting her! Stop. We are hurting her!" I pleaded.

"Jena, we have to get your mom to the hospital. I know she's hurting, but we have to get her to the doctor now. Let's keep going. Come on, Jena. You can do it. We're helping your mom."

It took us about five minutes to go a hundred feet, but we finally got Mom in Linda's front seat. I jumped in the back, still in my pajamas, and we were off. About fifteen minutes later, we pulled up to the ER. Linda ran in to get help, and three people came running out with a stretcher to get my mom.

Once they were wheeling her inside, I just lost it. I began to sob uncontrollably in the back seat. *God, I am begging you to see my mom right now. She's hurting so bad, and I don't know what's wrong, and I'm so scared she's going to die. Please, God, don't let my mom die. I can't live without my mom. Please, God, it's killing me to see her hurting so bad. God, please. Please help my mom. Please take away her pain and please heal my mom. Please, God.*

I didn't realize that I was talking out loud until I removed my hands from my face to wipe my tears and saw Aunt Linda looking in at me. Tears were falling down her face too, and she opened my door and pulled me close and hugged me so tight.

"Jena, God's not going to let your mom die. I just know it. I don't know how I know it, but I just do. Your mom is the sweetest lady in the world. God is going to take good care of her, okay? Try not to worry. I know that's really hard. But she's with the doctors now, and they are going to help her, Jena. I just know it. Come on, let's go inside, okay?"

Aunt Linda held my hand and led me inside. She found a seat for me to sit in and told me to wait there while she went to find the doctor. I don't know how long I sat there before Aunt Linda came back and got me.

"Come on, sweetie, let's go get you something to eat."

"I'm not hungry."

"I know, Jena, but let's just go to the cafeteria and find you some hot chocolate to sip on, alright?"

I felt numb. I didn't know what was going on. I didn't know what had happened to my Mom. I didn't know why my dad wasn't here. I didn't even know where Nate was. I guessed he got on the bus because he didn't know what was happening, but I really didn't know. I was so full of fear, a fear that put all the other fear I'd ever felt to shame. I'd never known a fear like this one. I couldn't lose my mom. I just couldn't lose my mom. The idea of that was agonizing.

The cafeteria was really noisy, and there were a lot of people there. Aunt Linda found a booth way in the back where no one else was and went to find us something to eat.

She came back with a tray full of stuff, but I still wasn't hungry. Not even a little bit. I could smell the hot chocolate, though, and that sounded good. She slid it over to me, and it felt really good going down. I hadn't realized I was chilly until I started drinking it. I'd forgotten that I was in my nightgown and didn't have any shoes on. The cafeteria was pretty cold. Aunt Linda told me to sit tight while she went to find me a blanket. When she came back with a blanket and some slippers, I was able to warm up in no time.

"Jena, I know you're really scared right now, and I understand, but do you think it would be okay if I asked you some questions? Do you think that would be okay?"

I nodded yes.

"When did your mom get sick?"

"I don't know. She was fine last night when Nate and I went to bed. She wasn't sick at all."

"Were your mom and dad fighting last night?"

"No. Everything was okay." Her question made me wonder if she knew about my dad hurting us. I wondered if my mom had told her. My mom and Aunt Linda were good friends. It sure sounded like she knew. But I was too scared to talk about that stuff. I didn't want things to get any worse for my mom, and right now she was the most vulnerable I'd ever seen her. And I was afraid to make my dad mad since he would have to take care of her.

"Are you sure, Jena? There is nothing you can think of at all that might be why your mom is in such pain?"

"No. I really can't. I would tell you."

Then I remembered...the drink. My Dad had tried to make my mom have a drink with him last night when Nate and I were going to bed. And my mom didn't drink. And even when she did, she didn't drink whiskey. Could the whiskey have made her this sick? No. It couldn't have. My dad drank it like water, and he never got sick like this. I just didn't know. And I didn't know whether to tell Aunt Linda about the drink or not. But I wanted to help my mom.

Could my dad have done something to her drink? Had he

poisoned it? No. Even he wouldn't do that. Would he?

"Jena? Are you done with your hot chocolate?"

I nodded. "Thank you."

"You're welcome. Why don't we go check on your mom now?"

I followed her back through the maze of halls, but my mind was far away. *God, did my dad poison my mom? Is that why he tried to make her drink such a strong drink that she wouldn't normally drink? So she wouldn't notice the taste? God, did he?*

My mind got stuck there. And my gut was telling me that's exactly what had happened. Which is also why he wouldn't let me call 911. I think my dad was hoping by the time Aunt Linda got to the house that my mom would be dead. And he just left me there with her. He left me alone with my mom, who he thought was dying. *God, no. Please don't let this be true. God, I can't look at it. Please, God. That's pure evil. And he just left me there with her knowing that I was in agony over seeing my mom in such pain. He just left me there.*

God, what do I do? Do I tell someone? Do I? What if they tell him what I said? I have to go home with him. What if he kills me for telling? Is he planning to poison Nate and me too? God, you have to tell me what to do because I don't know! If he poisoned her, will the doctors find it on their own? Why else would she be so sick? That's not the flu. And why isn't my dad here? God, I think that's the most telling thing of all. If your wife is so sick that she can't talk and she can't move, do you just walk out and leave her there? No, God. No one would do that. No one that wanted to make sure their wife was okay. He did it. He tried to kill my mom. And you let him. You can't let him get away with this! God, why aren't you protecting us? Am I supposed to tell someone what I think happened? Are you waiting for me? Please, God, you have to tell me what to do!

And all the missing pieces of the puzzle began to fall into place. Dad took Nate and me to meet his girlfriend. He threatened me into silence to not tell Mom about it. Less than a month later, my mom gets really sick. He did it. He did this. My dad tried to kill my mom. I had to do something. I had to. But what? My heart was pounding out of my chest. So many thoughts raced through my mind. What if my dad came here to see her? I couldn't leave him alone with her. He might do something else to her if she was getting better. I wondered if my mom knew what had happened to her? And if she had to stay here for a while then that left Nate and me alone with him. Was he going to hurt us too? Probably not because that would point to him as the guilty party. But how could I just go home with him, knowing he'd tried to kill my mom?

I couldn't tell him that I knew. I'd have to pretend that I had no idea what had happened to keep Mom and Nate safe. But if Mom was okay, we couldn't just go back home with him and act like nothing had happened. If he was willing to go this far then we'd never be safe again. *God, please tell me what to do. Do I tell? Will the police take him to jail so we will be safe? You are going to have to tell me what to do!*

Aunt Linda had me sit down in the ER lobby while she tried to get an update on Mom. As I was sitting there thinking about what to do, I saw Aunt Renee walk through the door. I was so happy to see her. She ran over and hugged me and kissed the top of my head.

"Jena, your Aunt Linda called me about your mama. How is she doing? Is she okay?"

"I don't know. No one has told me anything yet."

"Well, darling, you just sit right back down and I'm gonna go find out exactly what's going on!"

As she disappeared past the nurses' station, I sat back down in the cold hard yellow chair. Ten minutes later Aunt Renee returned. She sat down beside me and put her arm around my shoulder, pulled me into her, kissed my head like she always did, and said, "Your mama is going to be just fine! She's pretty sick right now and she sure doesn't feel too good, but the doctors said that she will make a full recovery! Isn't that wonderful, Jena!"

Tears of joy streamed down my face, and I nodded because I knew I couldn't speak without bursting into sobs again. But this time it was tears of gratitude that God saw my mom in her moment of greatest need and he helped her. He saved her. And in doing so, he saved me. I just wanted to hug God so badly. I hugged God inside my head, believe me. *Thank you, God. Thank you.*

"What is wrong with her?" I asked.

"They don't rightly know, Jena. They aren't sure yet. But I'm sure they'll figure it out soon. Don't worry."

I sure hoped Aunt Renee was right. I hoped they did figure it out. Surely, we wouldn't have to live with him anymore if they did. If she was poisoned, they'd know it was him. Who else would it be?

Mom was in the hospital most of that week, and Nate and I had to stay at home with Dad. I walked on eggshells that week and made sure I didn't say or do anything that would get him going. But I also paid even closer attention to his behavior than I normally did. I was searching for any sign or evidence that he had harmed my mom. He didn't give anything away, though.

When my mom finally did come home, Aunt Linda came and stayed with us for another week just to help out while Mom was getting her strength back. We were told it was hepatitis and we even had to get a shot. I didn't know what that was even after it was explained to me. But I didn't believe it. I knew what had happened, and it had nothing to do with whatever hepatitis was.

Two weeks later, after Mom had been back to the doctor for a follow-up visit, she received a phone call at the house, and I overheard my Mom say, "Well, if I don't have hepatitis, then what was it?" My heart fell into my stomach. I knew it! It really was true. My dad had caused my mom to get so sick. My dad had tried to murder my mom!

When she got off the phone, I went in to see what she was doing. She was sitting down at the eat-in table, resting her head in her hands.

"Mom? Is everything okay?"

She looked up and reached for my hand. "Yes, honey. Everything is fine. Are you hungry?"

"No thanks, Mom. Who was that on the phone?"

"Oh, just the doctor checking up on me."

"Mom?"

"Yes, Jena?"

"I heard you say that you don't have hepatitis."

"Oh. Well, yes, it sounds like it was something else after all. But let's not talk about that anymore, Jena, okay? I'm fine now, and that's all that matters. Right?"

"Okay, Mom," I reluctantly agreed. But I wanted to blurt out the obvious and just beg her to take Nate and me and run.

I was sure that she suspected the same thing that I'd known all along. What she didn't know is that she only had a partial picture of everything that was going on. If she had known about Dad's girlfriend, she would have had the same certainty as me that he was responsible for her illness.

Which left Nate and me as the only two people who could put it all together. Except Nate still believed Mom had hepatitis. And I was going to let him keep believing that because I had some really important things to figure out. Were we safer now because this had happened and my dad was under scrutiny, or was the writing on the wall and it was only a matter of time until he tried to hurt my mom again? I didn't know. But I felt immense pressure to figure it out. That sinking feeling was back that told me that my dad had to die in order for us to ever really be safe. And I hated that notion. Really hated it. It felt much easier to ask God to do away with my dad than to think of doing it myself. In my mind, I thought if God did it then it was justice, but if I did it, it was murder. It would be justifiable murder, self-defense for sure, but still murder and I didn't see myself as someone capable of that. And I felt guilty for even thinking this way right after God had saved my mom. It felt like I was dishonoring what God had done for me. But desperate people think, and sometimes do, desperate things.

Chapter 8

Just Do It, Jena!

Two months had passed since my mom was sick, and while I was still wrestling weekly with the thought of ending my father's life, I hadn't been able to move myself into action. It wasn't a little thing I was contemplating. And though my father's drunken binges hadn't let up, the physical abuse to my mom had been the lightest it had ever been. I wondered if that was out of a sense of guilt he felt for trying to kill her or if he was just afraid that people outside our home were onto him. Whatever the reason for the break, I was glad.

But then one night my dad got home really late. Despite all his other faults, my dad was always really reliable as far as his time commitments went. He was always home every night for dinner, right at 5:30 sharp. And on the rare occasion he was going to be late, he always called my mom and let her know. Sounded like a person who loved his home life so much he didn't want to miss a minute more of it than was necessary. But since we all knew that didn't describe my dad, I often thought he rushed home to make sure we were still all the weak little minions he'd left earlier in the day. Like he rushed home out of fear one of us had decided to tell the world who he really was. Whatever his reasons were, it was more than odd that my dad still wasn't home at 8 p.m. Had God finally decided to answer my prayers and let him die in a car accident? I didn't want to let myself hope, so I pushed that thought away.

At half past nine, he stumbled through the door. He was so drunk that I couldn't imagine how he had driven. I never understood how he never got pulled over, but he didn't, not even once! Or how he didn't get in an accident. I would always pray that if God did let him have an accident that he would be the only one that got hurt. I thought it was so wrong that my dad was taking chances with other people's lives every time he drove drunk. But it was a way of life for him. Since he was virtually always drunk or working on being drunk, if he was driving, he was intoxicated.

"Where the hell is my supper!" he slurred.

Immediately, Nate, Mom, and I were on high alert. Wherever this was going, it wasn't going to be good. My first thought was to pour him another drink. He was so drunk that with another drink or two, he'd pass out and we'd be safe. Problem was, I was forever pouring half of his whiskey bottles down the sink and replacing the balance with water, so it took more than usual to get him there. I couldn't count the times my mom had caught me doing this and had warned me not to get caught. I never did as far as I knew. He never said anything.

"Hi, Dad! I'll get it. Why don't you go change clothes and I'll have it ready?" I said as upbeat as I could.

I couldn't stand to be nice to my dad, but I found that it helped our cause sometimes, so I was willing to do it. My mom had started to come out of the kitchen, and I met her halfway and waved her back in. "Mom, he is really drunk. Just let me get him something to eat and fix him a drink so he passes out."

"Jena," my mom said hesitantly, "why don't you just go to the rec room and let me handle this?"

"No, Mom, it goes better when I do it. Please just go in the rec room. Go."

As Mom headed to the rec room with Nate, I warmed up the leftovers from dinner in the microwave for my dad, and I fixed him a huge whiskey with coke so he couldn't tell it was watered down. If ever there had been a night that I wished I hadn't watered it down, that was the night. But I thought the glass I fixed was big enough to do the trick.

By the time he practically fell through the kitchen door, I had his dinner on the table along with his drink.

"Why, thank you, Jena. That's awwwwwfulllly kind of you."

"You're welcome, Dad. I'll sit with you while you eat. Did you have a good day?" Oh, why did I just ask that? That was stupid.

"No, Jena. No, I certainly did not have a good day. Any more questions you'd like to ask?"

"Sorry, Dad. No. Guess what? I'm in the paper again. Want to read it?"

"Well, I'll just bet you are, Jena! You're always in the paper for somethin', now aren't ya! That's my girl. That's my girl."

Though I did have a lot of sports write-ups in the local paper, I never bragged about them. I never even mentioned them to anyone unless I was trying to put my dad in a good enough mood that he didn't hurt any of us. And sometimes it worked. Sometimes I could keep his focus on things he loved to talk about and think about until he passed out. I worked really hard to do that every single night.

It seemed to make Nate mad at me because he didn't understand what I was doing. He thought I was just bragging about myself to Dad or trying to make Dad like me better than him, which made Nate feel bad. I wished he could understand I did it for all of us. How could he possibly think I really wanted to put my hair in ponytails like a five-year-old and sit there and talk nicely to this person that hurt us all so badly? It was clear he didn't get it, but I couldn't let that bother me because what I was doing was far more important than any of our misunderstood feelings. We could sort all of that out if we survived.

The only time that Nate didn't mind me buttering Dad up was on the weekends when he wanted me to call Dad at work and ask him to bring us home some cookies or ice cream. And while I got the same sick feeling in my stomach as I always did when I pretended to be nice to my dad, I usually did it anyway. I think it's hard for anyone who isn't hostage to this type of long-term abuse to understand how manipulative the captives can become just to try to secure for themselves the simplest of decencies or wants. Because there was no other way to ever have anything that was good. My dad was never going to just offer something good out of the kindness of his heart; at least not to the three of us.

"All righty, Jena, that sure was good! Where's your mama? I haven't seen her this whole time I've been home! Wendy…Wendy!

Get your ass in here! Don't you know I'm home?" He got up to leave the table and had to grab the tabletop to steady himself.

"Dad, do you want dessert? Mom made a pumpkin pie. I can get you a piece."

"No, no, Jena, I'm not hungry. Where's your Mom?"

I didn't really want to fix him some pie, but I wanted him to finish drinking the drink I made him, and it was still half full.

I heard the rec room door open and saw Mom coming into the kitchen. She came over to my dad and kissed him on the lips, which was customary for them when he got home, unless he was already in a rampage.

"Richard," my mom said in greeting.

"Richard what? I've been home for an hour now and you're just now coming to see me! What the hell is that about? That's not acceptable. That's not acceptable at all," he slurred.

He'd only been home twenty minutes tops. Here we go, I thought to myself.

"Well, Jena wanted to spend time with her dad, and I wanted to let her do that, Richard. Wasn't that very sweet of her to fix your dinner for you?"

My dad rolled his head over to me and then back to my mom. He was so drunk that he was swaying, and I was just praying that he fell down before he could land a blow. But like a predator to its prey, my dad moved in on my mom in such startling fashion that I about jumped out of my skin. I didn't see it coming, it happened so fast.

He swung at her but missed and with his body in forward motion, he fell into her and knocked her to the kitchen floor, falling right on top of her. I quickly got behind him and wrapped my arms around his chest and pulled backward with all my might, but he already had a tight grip around my mom's neck. I moved my arms up around his neck and jumped backward with the weight of my body and it jerked him off of her. Mom scrambled to her feet and yelled for me to get to my room. That was a waste of breath because she knew I wasn't going anywhere.

As he tried to get to his feet, he reached behind himself, swatting at me, trying to make me release him, but I didn't budge. I knew if I let him up, he'd just go after Mom again. And it was only when he was this drunk that I even stood a chance of fending him off. I still had to use all of my strength and body weight, but he had so few faculties left about him that I could manage it if it didn't go on for too long.

He swatted at me for a few minutes and then lost steam. He slumped forward, but he was still in a kneeling position. I hoped he had passed out, but he could have been tricking me into letting go, so I hung on a little longer. When I finally decided he wasn't faking, I let go. He was passed out right there in a kneeling position on the kitchen floor.

"Jena, come on, let's go. Come on, now," my mom whispered.

Nate was already in his room, so Mom joined me in her room. I told her I was going to lie down on the floor on her side of the bed. She nodded. While Mom was in the bathroom getting changed for bed, I had a thought that I tried to push away, but it kept coming back. Maybe tonight is… maybe tonight I can… but I was unable to finish the thought even in my head. Mom climbed into bed, told me she loved me, and said goodnight. I wasn't sure how she could sleep when we didn't know what he was going to do next, but I understood too that when you lived this life, you had to steal moments of sleep when you felt it was the safest to do so, and with him passed out, even in a kneeling position, it was unlikely he'd have the endurance to do anything to us tonight. Which made it just the right time to…get rid of him.

After laying there on the floor with my mind racing for over an hour, I decided to sneak out to the kitchen and see if my dad was still there. My mom was already asleep, so I very quietly got up and tiptoed through the house to the kitchen. I was startled when I didn't see him there on the kitchen floor, and instantly I was afraid. Where was he? I quickly looked all around me, and I didn't see him anywhere. I knew he wasn't in the living room because I passed through there to get to the kitchen. That only left the rec room. I peeked through the glass on the rec room door, and sure enough, he was lying face down on the big sectional couch. I started to open the door, and it creaked so I froze to see if he'd heard me. He hadn't, so I opened it all the way and made my way slowly over to the back of the couch. I was behind him so if he was awake, he wouldn't see me. I looked around the room and spotted the fireplace poker on the hearth, and in that second, I knew what I was going to do.

I moved as silently as I could over to the front of the couch so I was facing him. I could see he was completely passed out but still had the drink in his hand. I didn't even know how that was possible. How could he be out cold but still be holding that glass?

It made no sense, but he was definitely out. I tested that theory by carefully removing the drink from his grip, which was easy to do; it practically fell into my hands. I set it down on the carpet and just stood there looking at him. I'd look at him then the poker then the clock, then him, the poker, the clock. This went on forever. *Just do it, Jena*, I kept telling myself. I tried to picture what was going to happen. I tried to visualize what I needed to do. *Just pick it up and with all your might, Jena, slam it through his head.* That's what I kept telling myself, over and over. By now, forty-two minutes had ticked off according to the clock sitting on the far side of the rec room behind the couch. Forty-two minutes. I was so angry with myself. I willed myself to do it for another twenty minutes, but in the end, I just couldn't reach for the poker. I couldn't do it. I couldn't kill my dad. I wanted more than anything in this world for my mom to finally be safe, for Nate and me to be safe. But I couldn't kill my dad to ensure our safety. It just wasn't in me. I looked at him one last time and thought to myself, I just can't do it.

I was relieved, but I also felt completely defeated. If I couldn't kill him and God wasn't going to, that meant we were going to keep living like this until he killed one of us. I didn't know how to accept that truth, but I knew it was the truth. And I felt like a bigger failure than I'd ever felt in my life. *God, why can't I do what needs to be done to save us? Why?* The tears started to fall. And they fell and fell and fell until I faded to black on my Mom's bedroom floor.

Next thing I knew, I woke to my dad tapping my foot with his.

"Jena, what are you doing? Wake up. You need to move so I can get in the closet or I'll be late for work. Come on. Let's go, sleepyhead! What are you doing down there anyway? You do know you have a bedroom right?" He smiled at me. I noticed he was still wearing the clothes he'd had on last night. I wasn't sure if he had slept the night through in the rec room or if he had come to bed at some point.

But the very first thing I thought when I saw him was that I was glad. Glad that he was still here. Glad I hadn't hurt him. Glad I hadn't killed him. What a bizarre thing to feel, was my second thought. As I shuffled to my feet, I could see that Mom was not in bed anymore. My Dad must have read my mind as he offered, "Mom's in the kitchen fixing breakfast. Why don't you go eat for a change?"

"Okay," I said, though I had no intention of eating breakfast. I hadn't eaten breakfast in so many years that I couldn't even remember when I'd stopped. I was always too unsettled in the morning to eat. My stomach was always in knots. But I did want to go see if Mom was okay, so I made my way to the kitchen. She was standing over the griddle making pancakes.

"Hi, Mom," I said.

"Good morning, Jena. I'd ask you if you want a pancake but I already know the answer, don't I? Hmmm?"

"No thanks, Mom, I'm good."

And just like that, just like every morning after the storm, we all pretended that nothing had happened. As I stood there leaning against the kitchen counter watching my Mom flip her perfect pancakes, I thought, *God, I'll never understand this crazy life you allowed me be to be born into, but one thing is for sure, I wouldn't trade having this mom for anything in the world. Even if it means having him for a dad.* And with that, I was content to head back down the hall and get ready for school.

Chapter 9

These Three

I used to wonder if there was going to be anything left of me if I did survive my dad. I wasn't so sure. For years, he'd done his best to make us feel worthless. He reinforced over and over that our only worth was in the things we did that reflected well on him. And he took credit for all of those things. And because we were so desperate for any kind of positive attention or personal acknowledgment, we learned to value and measure ourselves by the same standard.

This was never more evident to me than the day in Ms. Stanton's English class when she asked us to get out a piece of paper and write a mini autobiography. She said our assignment was to tell her who we were as people and describe ourselves so well that a stranger who'd never met us could read it and feel like we were old friends. To this day, I can remember the burning feeling in my stomach and the anxiety I felt.

As I glanced around, I saw my classmates writing furiously while my sheet of paper sat on my desk completely blank. This was a strange place to find myself. Usually her writing assignments would just spill out of me, and I'd have far more pages than she requested. But not this time. I couldn't get beyond, "My name is Jena Parks." What else was there to say? I really didn't know. I racked my brain trying to think of things I could say that would tell Ms. Stanton who I was. But I had nothing. And the only things I could come up with I didn't dare put in writing. My paper would have read:

My name is Jena Parks. I'm scared all the time. Of everything. My greatest fear is that my dad will someday kill my mom in a drunken rage. And that thought has consumed every waking moment of my life for fifteen years. You can't begin to imagine how tired I am. My dad's a raging alcoholic who beats us all the time. He's also a cheater and flaunts his girlfriend in front of my brother and me. My mom has no idea he's betraying her this way. Beyond that, there's not much else to say. I can run really fast but I hate to run. My dad makes me do it. The only real conversations I've ever had in my entire life are with God. No one else knows a single thing about my life. No one knows me. Including me.

After fifteen minutes of sitting there with an empty piece of paper, I headed up to Ms. Stanton's desk and told her I didn't feel well and asked if I could go to the bathroom. She said yes and handed me a hall pass. I didn't come back for the rest of the class. Ms. Stanton sent another student in to check on me, and I told her my stomach hurt and that I would be in there for a while. When I heard the bell ring, I made my way back to class to collect my things. Ms. Stanton asked me if I was okay and if I needed to go to the office and call home. I assured her I would be fine, that I was just a little nauseated. As I turned to leave, she reminded me to finish my paper and bring it to the next class to read out loud. I nodded in agreement, but I never completed that assignment, I took a zero on it in a class where I normally held straight A's.

For me that simple writing assignment was a reality check. Up till that point, I hadn't stopped to think about who I was; I was too busy trying to survive my circumstances. But it forced me to think about those things. Look at those things. I realized I wasn't being raised to see myself as an individual, as someone of value or worth with plans or desires of my own. In our home, we were all there to serve only one purpose: to submit our will fully to Dad's. We were props, there to make him look good. And only he could decide in what capacity that would be. For me, I'd come to learn I was to look pretty, run fast, and win awards. I was to be silent unless spoken to and to comply at all times with a smile on my face. I could only consistently manage the ones that were God-given abilities. I failed miserably at the others. The more exposure I had to my teachers and other students in high school, the more I began to understand just how different our lives were compared to everyone else's.

Every morning when I arrived at school, I felt an extra surge of anxiety. I didn't know why, but I'd felt this way since kindergarten. It was partially tied to everything that went on at home, but it was more than that. It was so hard to step into a world every day that you didn't feel connected to. And let's face it, high school is no joke. Some of the cruelest people you'll ever meet roam those halls. I don't think parents realize how vicious kids can be to one another.

And while no one had ever successfully bullied me, I was often on the receiving end of the dumbest stuff ever from other girls in the school. Just pure mean-girl nonsense. It was probably just normal stuff everyone dealt with at that age, but because my world was so much more complicated than worrying about who was wearing what and who was dating whom and who said what to whom, I couldn't stand to be there. I couldn't relate to most of what was going on around me. I toggled between being so irritated I just wanted to scream "Please just shut up!" and wishing that my world was as carefree as theirs, so I too was consumed only by immature, juvenile realities. I was pretty sure they were right where they were supposed to be, thinking exactly what they were supposed to be thinking. It was me that was off. Way off. It was me that couldn't relate to the innocence or the simplicity of their world.

I don't know, maybe it's hard to like what you don't know. I logged some serious hours trying to figure out why people didn't seem to really "like" me. Sounds contradictory that you could be considered one of the most popular girls in the school and also be one of the most misunderstood and disliked. I think it was because I built walls to protect myself at a very young age, and I hadn't allowed myself to ever be vulnerable. It was the only way to survive the kind of constant abuse we suffered at home. And then when you're out in the real world, that persona follows you. It becomes who you are. And you don't know how to let your guard down and let people in. You can't expect people to know who you are when you're all locked up inside your own head and heart. I often heard my classmates whisper, "She's so stuck up," as I passed by. And I'd think, *Who the hell are they talking about? What does that even mean? I'm the last person in the world who would think I have anything to be stuck up about.*

Are you kidding me? What's to covet about my life? Nothing. Not one thing.

But again, this is where perception is so flawed. And let's face it, people see what they want to see. And not much more. That person was who my classmates wanted me to be. Everyone enjoys gossiping about the villain. But I just wasn't her. I wasn't the villain. I was the girl stuck living inside my own head, inside my own pain, that so badly wanted to connect with others. The one that so badly wanted to feel kindness from others. But I was always holding so much back. And holding so much in. I just couldn't reach out. And I couldn't be reached. Eventually you believe your only viable option is to just not care. And that's a slippery slope, a dangerous conclusion to come to. Pretend not to care long enough and eventually you won't.

Fortunately, God intervenes on our behalf sometimes, and he certainly did that with me many, many times when I'd chosen a path of total mental and emotional isolation from the human race. Throughout those troubling high school years, he sent me three of the best people I could have ever hoped to call friends: Kelsey Melton, Samantha Garner, and Eric Fox. The three of them could not have been more different from one another, but each one shined a unique light and love into my life that I desperately needed.

Kelsey was the most well-liked person in the entire school and one of the most naturally pretty girls you've ever seen. No makeup at all and she was just flawless, her skin perfect. I used to say she was as pretty on the outside as she was on the inside. You couldn't help but like Kelsey. And she had the most beautiful smile you've ever seen, with a laugh that was so infectious it made everyone want to be around her. There was a light around Kelsey, just this glow about her that made her stand out from the crowd. Kelsey was ridiculously popular with the boys and the girls. She had at least as many guy friends as she did girlfriends. And Kelsey was a star athlete; there wasn't a sport that this girl didn't excel in. She and I became friends through our love of sports, and though I was a year older than Kelsey, we were often on the same team. We became an unstoppable duo on the basketball court. We had a natural rhythm where we knew where the other was going to be before we even got there. Playing basketball with Kelsey was by far the most fun I ever had during my high school years. I was our point guard, known throughout the district for playing stifling defense, averaging 18 steals a game, while Kelsey was a brilliant shooter and leading scorer in the district, averaging 22 points a game. She could shoot from anywhere—inside, outside, didn't matter. And it was a smooth shot at that. Just so pretty. The only sport where I could best Kelsey was track and field. We would joke about that all the time. I'd tell her that someone had to keep her humble. While Kelsey and I bonded over sports, our friendship ran much deeper. Once I met her family, I realized that it was our shared belief in and love of God that led us to connect the way that we did.

Kelsey's mom was the most special person I'd ever met outside of my own mother. And once I met her, I could see where Kelsey got all of her amazing qualities. Mrs. Melton would come to be the angel looking out for me, the encourager and supporter that I never had in my own home, and the one person that would go to bat for me with teachers and coaches when I couldn't stand up for myself. While I never told Kelsey or her mom about my struggles at home, I knew that Mrs. Melton could see the pain in me, and she so genuinely wanted to ease my burden. She loved a child that wasn't her own, and she lifted me when I needed it the most. For that, I will forever be grateful. In my mind, there is no question that God brought Kelsey and me together because he knew how much I needed to know what love felt like. Not the kind of love I was used to where you had to earn it through what you could do. No, Kelsey and Mrs. Melton loved me for me, and they accepted me right where I was, not expecting or demanding me to be more than I could be. It brings me to tears still when I think about how their love lifted me at a time and place when I desperately needed it.

Samantha Garner was as loud as Kelsey was mild mannered. She was something else, that girl. A transfer into my grade from our rival school, Samantha came in completely unafraid and unapologetic about who she was or how she did things. She was boisterous. She was defiant. She was fun. Oh my gosh, was Samantha fun. She was a bit of a rebel, though, compared to the rest of us. She had transferred from a school where shrinking violets would be chewed up and spit out. In the beginning, I thought that was why she was so bold. I'd later come to realize that was just Samantha's natural disposition. We were an unlikely pair, and people felt the need to point that out to me all the time. I'd get asked all the time why Samantha and I were friends. I couldn't explain it to others. I was so private and guarded and she was so outgoing. I was quiet and she was so bold and in your face. But I adored Samantha. And she was good for me. And, well, she was bad for me. But mostly good. She brought me to life in so many ways. Samantha's spark and

I-don't-give-a-damn-what-anyone-thinks attitude helped pull me outside of my own head and allowed me to live a little. I felt free when I was with Samantha. And she never made me feel bad about myself when I'd retreat inside my own little world. And because Samantha was so unafraid to express herself at all times, it helped me to be able to say the things out loud that I would typically keep bottled up inside my own head.

Samantha loved the boys. And they loved her. Samantha was an edgy rocker-type brunette with a tall, slender figure and huge brown eyes. She was a pretty girl. Samantha did not lack attention from the opposite sex, and she was very affectionate in her relationships. I, on the other hand, had zero experience in that area. I was still afraid of that kind of stuff and had declared years prior that I wasn't having sex until I was married. I didn't know if that was a God thing or a protection thing or both. My view of the opposite sex had been shaped by my dad, and it certainly wasn't a good impression I had of them. So I spent a lot of time running from boys and relationships. Particularly with Jason, who was two years older than me and pursued me relentlessly for years. No matter what I threw at Jason, telling him I wasn't having sex until I was married or that I didn't have any time to spend with him, no matter what I said to him, he was undeterred and determined that we were going to date. So Samantha and I were polar opposites in this way. But regardless of our differences, we had each other's backs to the very end. If you had a problem with her, you had a problem with me and vice versa.

And then there was Eric Fox. I could go on forever about Eric.

We had gone to school together since elementary school but didn't become good friends until high school. We bonded over our love for 80s hair bands. We were both so into that music scene, and Eric looked every bit the part, which was such a contradiction to who he was. Eric was the sweetest, kindest, funniest guy one could ever hope to meet and so handsome. He had long gorgeous hair, piercing blue eyes, and a killer smile. Yet he was the humblest guy ever, shy in many ways. He really had no clue how amazing he was, which was one of the things that made him so special. Eric and I became fast friends our sophomore year and were pretty much inseparable from that point on. He and Samantha would sometimes bicker with each other, but I'd just stay out of it. I think Eric thought at times that Samantha was going to get me in trouble. But we worked our way through the kinks as best we could, and I was honored to call both of them friends.

I shared more of myself with these three people than anyone else in my life; yet, I never told any of them what I was dealing with at home. I don't know why. I think it was different things at different times. I was ashamed. I was afraid of what would happen if I told, especially if Mrs. Melton found out. Oh, she would not have stood for that. Something would have happened, that's for sure. And I think that even though I had strong urges at times to tell each of them, the greater urge was to protect Nate and my mom from what might happen if I told.

Kelsey, Samantha, and Eric were the only semblance of normalcy in my life during those years. They were such good friends to me, and each brought a unique love and joy into my otherwise dismal, hopeless existence. And though I know each one of them could sense a heaviness in me, could see I was being weighed down by something, they never pushed me to talk about it, and they never judged me for how I was different. Each one of them was an incredible blessing in my otherwise cursed my life.

Chapter 10

You Want Me to Do What?

As the school week wound down, I looked forward to just being at home with my mom. While our weekends were hardly typical high school teenager weekends, I still looked forward to not having to leave my mom for extended periods of time. Weekends were definitely less anxiety ridden for me than Monday through Friday because I didn't have to wonder if my mom was okay. I was pretty much glued to her side until Monday morning rolled around.

Nate and I never had friends over to our house. We would never take a chance on someone seeing how we lived. We were so embarrassed by our dad's alcoholism and, obviously, it would be catastrophic if anyone from school saw what he did to us during his drunken rages.

From time to time, I would pull a book from the shelf of our school library on alcoholism and sneak it into the bathroom and read it sitting in the stall during lunch. I'd usually do this on Fridays so I had the weekend to think about what I'd read. I learned that alcoholism is a disease and that alcoholics are never cured of the disease, but rather they can live in a state of recovery if they get help. I never really thought of my dad as having a disease. I just looked at him as someone who liked to drink and would drink too much, which led to him being meaner than he usually was. I saw it as a choice. Not a disease. Probably the most disturbing thing that I read is that some alcoholics can't remember their actions when they're drunk. I wasn't sure how that worked because I hadn't been drunk before, but I knew one thing—the thought of that infuriated me.

But it did possibly explain why my dad was always so chipper the morning after he'd abused us. He truly acted as if nothing had happened. And we all just followed suit because, well, I don't know exactly why we followed suit like such good little minions, but I think it's because you cling to any moment that seems stable. And you try to hang onto it and extend it for as long as possible. Because you know it's only a matter of time before the darkness sets in again. So maybe my dad didn't remember all of the unspeakable acts he'd committed against us. I don't know. Maybe I'll never know. But the idea of it didn't sit well with me. It might be his disease, but it made us all sick; we all suffered because of it. And his impairment impaired us too. I didn't see any escape for Mom, Nate, and me.

I can't say that I ever felt better after reading through that library book, but I did gain a better understanding of what we were dealing with. I think the part I found the most discouraging is that it said you can't help an alcoholic get better; they have to decide to get better on their own. I didn't see that happening; my dad would likely never admit he had a problem…of any kind.

I was so happy when Sunday rolled around because I loved Sunday school and always learned something really helpful that I could apply to my life at home. I'm sure my Sunday school teacher thought my thirst for knowledge in class was admirable for a kid my age. She couldn't possibly know that what I learned there was my lifeline. I needed to know what God said because I was always searching for something that would reveal what God was going to do about our situation at home. But on this Sunday morning, I learned the most confusing thing. I thought that it couldn't be right, so I couldn't wait to get home and look up the verses myself and figure out what the teacher really meant to say.

My teacher said that God tells us that we are to pray for those who hurt us, that we are supposed to pray for our enemies. I immediately began a discussion with God in my head and just let him know right off the bat that I didn't think the teacher could possibly have that right. That would mean God wanted me—that God *expected* me—to pray *for* my dad? Why would I pray for someone who had never done anything but hurt me? Why in the world would I pray *for* the person that I thought was going to kill one of us someday?

All the way home, I was lost in thought. So much so that when my mom asked me and Nate if we wanted to get Slurpees from 7-11, I said no. And next to my mom's spaghetti, a Slurpee is surely my favorite thing on planet Earth. No, a Slurpee couldn't help me right now. I needed to get home and figure this thing out.

I did pray for my dad all the time. I prayed for him to die. I prayed for God to take him away. I prayed for him to get in a car accident. But that isn't the kind of praying my teacher was talking about. She said that we are to pray for good things for our enemies. Why in the world would I want something good for him when he clearly didn't want anything good for me? Why would I ever ask God to help him? He didn't deserve that!

I raced inside when we got home, grabbed the Bible off the shelf, and locked myself in my room. Luckily, there were tabs for each book in the Bible, so I found what I was looking for within seconds. Okay, let me see…there it…is…

Matthew 5:44: "But I tell you, love your enemies and pray for those who persecute you."

I kept reading, and God goes on to say that when the sun rises and sets, it does so on the good and evil. And when it rains, it rains on the good and evil. He says if all you do is love the people who love you, what good is that? What reward is there in that? All people do that. And he says he calls us to love our enemies the way he loves us.

I closed the Bible and held it across my chest as I lay there on my bed looking up at the ceiling. It felt like my mind stopped working for several minutes. I was staring so intently at the plaster patterns on the ceiling that they began to look like cracks. I didn't know what to think. Or to say. I now knew it was true, what my teacher had said. And I knew that's what God expected me to do. And I knew I couldn't do it. I didn't *want* to do it.

I'd found a way to be patient with God, though he never changed my circumstances at home. As baffled as I was by that, I never got angry with God. Even as a very young kid, I had figured out that God was far smarter and wiser than me. I could accept all of those things. But this? I didn't know how to accept this. And it was upsetting because I didn't want to let God down. I didn't want to tell him I couldn't do something he was asking me to do.

God, it's me Jena. I know you know what I'm thinking right now. And I'm sorry that I can't do it. But God, you have seen and heard everything my dad has ever done and said to us. How can I pray for him? I don't want to. Please don't be mad at me. I don't know how you expect me to feel any different than that. He's even tried to kill my mom. I may not have seen what he put in her drink that night with my own eyes, but I know he did it! And you want me to pray for him?

I lay there in silence a while longer, just hoping God would explain it to my heart like he often did. But nothing.

God, you're really mad at me, aren't you? I don't want you to be mad at me. You're all I have. And I need you. I really am sorry. But I can't tell you something that isn't true. You would know I'm lying. I just don't feel in my heart that I could ask you to help my dad. But I won't ask you to kill him anymore. I'll stop doing that.

And as I was saying those words, it hit me. All these years I had been asking God to sin in my prayers. I literally had been asking God over and over to kill my dad. I don't know why I never got it before. But now it was as plain as the nose on my face. I had been asking God, who can't sin, to commit sin…in order to help me. No wonder he never answered that prayer. And to think of how many hours I spent stumped that he didn't answer that specific prayer. What was I thinking? I don't know. I guess clarity and desperation don't necessarily go hand in hand.

I'm not sure how long I lay there sorting through all the discussions I'd had with God over the years, thinking about all the times I had pleaded with God to do something that was not in his nature to do. I apologized for each discovery and vowed not to do it again. I would have to learn a whole new way of talking to God. I never really called it praying, but I know that it was. It just always felt more like conversations with God because I thought of prayer as something more formal, where the words had to be arranged a certain way. I just poured out whatever was in my heart and on my mind at any given moment to God. That's what felt right to me. It was always a relationship in my mind. And I liked it that way.

Though my dad kept right on beating us, I kept my word. I never did ask God to let my dad die again. And I never thought about killing him again myself. But I did ask God to make him stop drinking. And I did ask God to convince him to leave us on his own accord, even if it was to go be with that other woman. I didn't care how he left, I just wanted him to leave so that we would be safe and so there would be no more suffering, pain, and fear.

But God has a way of working on those that love him to bring us around to where he wants us to be, where he can "prosper" us. The verse I clung to the most during my teenage years was Jeremiah 29:11: "For I know the plans I have for you, plans to prosper you and not to harm you, plans to give you hope and a future."

Though I rarely saw any evidence of that verse in my own life, I was drawn so strongly to it, and I believed it, even though I had no real proof yet that it was true.

But God slowly changed my heart that year by leading me to

think more and more about my dad as a person, separate from the alcoholism and separate from the abuse. He helped me to see him through different eyes by thinking of him as a child and about the horrific abuse he had suffered at the hands of his own father. And when I'd get the angriest at my dad or the most afraid of him, I'd force myself to remember that he was once in my shoes too. And I'd think about the fact that my dad had to quit school in the eighth grade to help his dad on the farm.

I couldn't fathom being made to quit school at such a young age and then having to figure out a way to survive or build a future beyond that. It must have been so hard. It led me to feel a sense of pride in my dad for what he had been able to accomplish, for the good things about him. And there were some good things about him. He was a really good custom home builder. He could draw the most incredible blueprints and floor plans with such great detail. I'd watch him sometimes from a distance, just fascinated that he could draw his idea on paper and then build it with his own two hands. It was pretty amazing. And working as the manager of a lumberyard helped him be able to build his homes as cost effectively as possible and then make a larger profit. My dad was the hardest worker I'd ever seen. He'd work from dusk till dawn between the farm, the lumberyard, and building homes for people on the side. My dad was a good provider. We always had what we needed in that regard.

And he could be kind and so generous. Never to us. But always to a stranger in need. Every single time I saw my dad help someone that was down on their luck, and there were too many to count, it would touch my heart. Yes, it would anger me too because I didn't understand how that much goodness could exist inside of him and yet he never showered it on the three people that were starving for it. But the anger didn't negate the contentment I felt seeing him extend a helping hand to someone so clearly in need. I loved that about my dad. And I longed to feel his kindness aimed at me. Even if it was just one time. I wanted to experience it.

There were many moments that I found genuine compassion for my dad, and tears. I began to picture him more and more at my age, wanting the same things that I so desperately wanted now. To be safe. To not be so afraid. To be loved. But my dad didn't feel any of those things as a kid either. And he didn't know how to give them to me. And it was during these moments, when I realized that my dad was every bit as tortured as I was, that I began to pray *for* him. I began to ask God to heal my dad's alcoholism and to give him peace because I knew how it felt to have none.

Bit by bit, I could feel God changing me from the inside out. He made me realize that I wasn't seeing the need in my dad any more than my dad was seeing the need in me. And it occurred to me that this was how this whole mess got started in the first place. And we were just passing it down from one generation to the next. I vowed that this cycle of abuse would end with me, one way or another. I had studied my dad so intently for so long. Surely, I could figure this out with God's help.

I began to rethink every conclusion I'd come to about my dad, just to see how intact they really were. I thought about how angry I'd get with him when he would talk about God and start crying. I think I felt like my dad wasn't entitled to God. And in my mind, the hypocrisy of it all was too much. I didn't understand how my dad—who beat us pretty much every day of our lives, verbally, physically, and sometimes both—could get so emotional talking about God when he clearly wasn't interested in doing what God said.

Or was he? Maybe he was. Maybe he got lost so long ago inside his own fear and anger that he felt helpless to find his way back. And of all the people in the world, couldn't I understand how that felt? While my childhood was mirroring my dad's to a large extent, there were some differences. My dad was forced to quit school in the eighth grade, and I was already in the tenth. I had spent countless hours thinking about our lives and our situation, analyzing it from every angle. My dad hadn't had time to do any of that. He'd gone to work on his dad's farm at the age of thirteen and had been working for his survival ever since. Did his inability to break this generational cycle of abuse mean that he didn't want to? Did it mean that he didn't know God or love God? No. It didn't. It just meant he hadn't found a way to overcome his circumstances. Instead, he repeated them.

Now I understood his tears when he talked about God. They were tears of guilt. Tears of sorrow. Tears because he felt powerless to change what he'd become. I started to understand so many things about my dad once I set aside my anger toward him. I couldn't help but think about how much harder it was for someone to break the cycle of abuse when they were born into it and it was all they had known versus someone like my mom. And I can definitely see the difference in my mom compared to Dad, Nate, and me. Even after everything she'd suffered at his hands, she was still so kind, gentle, and loving. She still trusted in people, believed in the good in them. She wasn't angry the way the three of us were. And she never said a bad word about anyone, including my dad. And she corrected me every time I spoke poorly about him. She wouldn't allow it.

Maybe that was subconsciously one of the reasons I fought so hard for her; not just because she was my mom, but to preserve that. Hoping maybe one day if we could get away from my dad, maybe, just maybe, she could help me find some of that goodness in myself. Maybe she could help me not be so afraid and not be so angry. Maybe I could learn to trust people too. I wanted to believe that. But if any of that was going to happen, I had to first make sure I didn't repeat the same mistakes my dad had, the same mistakes his father had. And that change in behavior, it had to start now. As hard as it was going to be, I had to try.

I was going to have to stop judging my dad so harshly. And if I wanted God to extend his grace and mercy to me, shouldn't I also want that for my dad? Didn't we both need it equally? I was beginning to understand that I couldn't commit a wrong to right a wrong.

I could begin to see now too how God had spared me a lifetime of remorse by not taking my dad from this earth when I begged him to. God knew my heart better than I did, and he knew I wouldn't be able to live with the guilt of believing I was responsible for his death. Besides, it wasn't for me to write the ending of my dad's story; only God could do that. And maybe, just maybe, he wasn't finished working in my dad's life yet either.

All that time that I thought God wasn't answering my prayers, that he wasn't helping me, he was actually very purposefully leading me to the appointed time and place of my rescue. He was shaping me into the person that he created me to be. And it's in the trenches and through the tragedies that God shapes our character. It's when all the chips are down and the storm is raging that we learn what we're made of. We discover who we are and, just as important, who we're not. I wasn't the kid that could carry the guilt of her dad's death. I wasn't the kid that could take her own father's life to spare another. And against every belief I had about myself, I was the kid that had it in her to lift my enemy up in prayer.

And I promised God that if one day he blessed me with children of my own, their lives would never be framed by violence but rather by unconditional love, protection, open communication, and nurturing.

By the time I was halfway through high school, God had completely renovated my heart and mind, and our talks were much deeper and more meaningful. My life, however, was as desperate as ever. And I still believed that unless God intervened, one of us was not going to make it out alive because there was such a progression in the severity of abuse we were suffering. And my dad was completely lost to his rage and alcohol most days.

And even though I knew in my gut it would eventually end tragically, I never could have imagined that it would be me that would end it.

Chapter 11

You're Never Going to Live Like This Again!

It started out like a typical Saturday night in our house. My dad had finished working on the farm and was starting to shift his focus to heavier drinking. My mom was preparing dinner, and I was setting the table for her like I did every night. Nate was planning to go spend the night at his best friend Steve's house as he'd been doing more and more of lately. Nate and I were opposites in that sense; I never wanted to be out of the house or away from my mom if I wasn't forced to be, and Nate couldn't wait to get out of the house. He jumped at every chance he could to vacate the premises. I can't say that I blamed him. It was torture to be there all the time, knowing how powerless you were to change anything.

Mom had made a delicious-smelling beef stew with onions, carrots, and potatoes and homemade biscuits. I couldn't wait to eat! As we passed the food around, my dad seemed to be in a decent mood and he allowed us to talk. Halfway through dinner, the old rotary phone hanging on the kitchen wall rang, and we all just looked at each other. It must be for Nate, I thought, because no one ever called for my mom except Grandma, and my dad rarely talked on the phone. As for me, if friends ever called for me, I always told my mom to say I wasn't there or that I was busy doing homework before she even picked up. I wasn't much of a phone talker, and I never wanted anyone from school to overhear my dad when he was drunk or angry, or both.

"Hello?" my dad said. "Who is this? Okay, just a minute."

"Jena, it's for you. Samantha…"

I wanted to shake my head no, but since it was my dad and not my mom, I decided the best thing to do was to take the call.

Feeling uneasy about having any conversation in front of my dad, I just said, "Hey…"

"When? Tonight? Ummmm. Well…I don't think…what? Ummm. Okay, hold on, I'll ask," I said as I put the phone receiver to my chest to muffle my voice.

"Mom, Dad…Samantha wants to know if I can go to a movie at the mall with her tonight? She said her mom would drive us and pick us up." I was praying the answer was no. I don't want to go anywhere, and I'm not sure why Samantha even asked me. She knew I didn't do anything on the weekends. It was like I disappeared Friday and was never seen again by anyone at school till Monday.

My dad piped up, "Sure, Jena, you can go. But tell Samantha to tell her mom that I'll drive you girls and pick you up."

My heart fell into the pit of my stomach. What in the heck was I going to do now?

"Dad, you don't have to—"

"Jena! Don't keep her holding. Tell her you can go and that I'll drive the two of you."

I lifted the receiver back to my mouth, but Samantha had already heard what my dad had said, "Great! Pick me up at seven, okay? See you then, it's going to be fun!"

I'd barely said okay before she hung up. I sat back down to finish dinner, though I wasn't nearly as hungry as before the phone rang, and I thought, what am I going to do now? All of a sudden, I had even more of a vested interest in how much my dad was drinking. Especially since he was going to be driving us.

It was like he read my mind because he got up from the table, dumped his drink in the sink, and got a glass of iced tea. It was 5 p.m., which meant we'd have to leave in an hour and a half. He wasn't drunk yet, but it was obvious to anyone paying close attention that he had been drinking. Hopefully, he had enough time to get back to normal before we left.

"Jena, you girls will have fun," my mom said. "I'm glad you're going. It will be good for you to get out of the house on a Saturday night."

I forced a smile, but no words followed. *I don't know what you're thinking, Mom, this is a horrible idea. I have to worry that Samantha will see my dad drinking or, worse yet, that her parents will see. I have to worry about what my dad will say during the ride there and back. He says the most inappropriate things and seems to be clueless that they are inappropriate. Oh, God, help me, this seriously stinks. Please let Samantha call me back and cancel. Please.*

But no such luck. Six thirty rolled around, and my dad yelled back to me from the kitchen, "Jena, come on, time to go!"

"Coming!" I yelled back so unenthusiastically.

My dad was holding the front door open when I rounded the corner. "Come on, come on, get the lead out. We have to get on the road so we're not late!"

My dad headed to his pickup truck, which struck me as odd because we'd all have to sit on the bench seat. I wondered why we weren't taking his company car, but I didn't dare ask. He knew where Samantha lived because we'd dropped her off once before. She was already waiting outside on the front porch when we pulled in her driveway, and she came bouncing down the path to the truck.

"Hey, guys! Hi, Mr. Parks!" Samantha says.

"Hi, Samantha. How are you?" my dad offered while I slid over to the middle seat right next to him.

"Good, thanks! Jena, you excited to see this movie? I am!"

I couldn't even remember what she said we were seeing, but I replied, "Yeah, definitely."

Thankfully, Samantha did all of the talking on the way to the mall because I didn't want my dad to talk, and I was too nervous to talk. When we pulled up to the curb, my dad told us to wait for him so he could pay for our tickets.

"Oh, you don't have to do that, Mr. Parks. I have money," Samantha said.

"Don't be silly. Your money's no good here. I'm paying," he insisted.

I just wanted him to leave, but instead we all filtered inside the mall entrance and over to the movie box office. It was 7:30, and the movie scroll showed that our movie started at 7:00. When Samantha realized she had gotten the times wrong, she apologized all over herself while my dad was just very quiet.

"Don't worry, sir. If the girls would like to go on in and watch the movie now, they are more than welcome to stay over for the next showing and catch the part they missed. They've only missed about fifteen minutes because the first fifteen minutes are previews," the manager offered.

"What do you girls want to do?" my dad asked but not in his good mood voice, more like his irritated voice.

"Let's just go ahead and watch it from here. We'll figure out what we missed, it's fine," Samantha offered.

"Okay," I said as I searched my dad's face to try to figure out what he didn't like about the situation.

"All right, well I will pick you girls up right after the movie, okay?" my dad said.

"Yeah, that's fine, we don't need to stay over and catch the beginning of the next one. See you when it's over. Thanks, Dad."

As my dad headed back outside, I wondered what he was thinking, but Samantha was already pulling me toward the concession stand to buy popcorn, drinks, and Twizzlers.

After a few minutes, I was able to focus on the movie and had a really good time. By the time it was over, I was glad Samantha had convinced me to go. She and I followed the crowd from the theater out into the mall; I looked left and right, but I didn't see my dad anywhere. I didn't really want to move from where we were standing, but Samantha said we should go look for him, so we walked up and down the mall once but didn't see him. I suggested we look outside for his truck, so we headed out to the parking lot and sure enough, his truck was there, but he wasn't in it. We headed back into the mall and saw my dad walking toward us from inside the mall.

"Hey, Mr. Parks!" Samantha beamed. "Great movie! Thanks for taking us!"

My dad nodded. Didn't say one word. Didn't acknowledge my friend had even spoken to him. He just nodded. Samantha didn't know—but I certainly did—that it was an angry nod. My stomach started doing flips and I felt the anxiety rise.

God, I don't know what's wrong, but please, please don't let him say or do anything in front of Samantha! Pleeeeeaaaasssse.

I tried to cover for the uncomfortable moment by talking nonstop to Samantha all the way home. She didn't seem to notice that anything was wrong, and when we got to her house, she thanked me and my dad and said she'd catch me at school on Monday.

She closed the door behind her, and I slid back over to where she had been sitting, relieved not to be sitting right up on my dad anymore. I didn't know if he had gone back home after he dropped us off or had just waited for us, but I could definitely tell that he had been drinking. I could smell it on him.

I waited on edge for him to say something, anything, but he didn't say one word to me all the way home. I knew I was in trouble, I just didn't know why. I hadn't done anything. But when did that ever matter? We pulled into our driveway, and all the lights were on, so I knew my mom was still up. I wasn't surprised; she never went to bed before my dad did. I don't think she was allowed to, as strange as that sounds.

"Hi, Jena, was it fun?" my mom said as I made my way through the door.

"Yeah, it was. Thanks, Mom," I said, still feeling really anxious.

My dad came through the door a few minutes behind me and headed straight for the back of the house. Then he yelled for my mom.

"Wendy! Get back here!"

My mind and body shifted into full panic mode. What was going on?

My mom glanced at me before heading down the hall, but she didn't say anything. I decided to follow behind her at a distance so she didn't know that I was following her, but I could hear what was said.

The door slammed as soon as my mom entered their bedroom and I moved closer.

"You know what?" he yelled. "Your daughter is as big a slut as you are!"

"Richard! Don't say things like—"

Before she could even finish her thought, I heard him slap her across the face and the door jolted as her body slammed into it. I reached for the knob, but it was locked. I had to get in there! I ran to the hall bathroom to grab a Q-tip, and I quickly broke it in half so I could use the solid end to open the door. I heard my dad's rant continue.

"She's a real piece of work, that one! She didn't go to the movie.

She and her slut friend snuck outside to go meet some boys. And you know damn well what they were doing! I saw them coming back inside the mall when I went to pick them up. That's your daughter!" he said.

Something happened to me after hearing him say those horrible things about me that I'd never heard him or anyone say before. And I saw red. My body began to shake, but not in fear, and I felt a heat through my whole body, like an intense adrenaline rush. I didn't feel in control of myself.

My mind raced, and I kept fumbling with and dropping the Q-tip on the ground because I couldn't think straight. Did he just call me a slut? A slut? Like my mom? A slut? I had never even kissed a boy, let alone done anything else! Everyone at school made fun of me for it, always calling me chicken and other names. The guys always joked that it was a waste of time to ask me out because they wouldn't get anywhere with me. And my own dad was calling me a slut?

By the time I could finally hold the Q-tip with a steady enough hand, my dad jerked open the door, pushed me out of the way, and stormed down the hall. My mom followed quickly but stopped to ask me what had happened. I told her that he was crazy and that I had no idea what he was talking about. I assured her we were in the movie the whole time and that the only time we went outside was to find him afterward. As I gave her the rundown, I got angrier and angrier, wondering why she was even questioning me. She knew me. She knew better. It was absurd for her to even ask me the question and it infuriated me. After all of the times I'd defended her and never once even considered that a single despicable thing he said about her had any merit to it, and now here she was actually considering that what he had just said about me could be true?! That would be like me questioning her about dad calling her a slut when I knew she'd only ever been with him. I mean it was just so damn ridiculous. The only slut in our house was my dad! By the time my mom asked her last question, I was operating on pure adrenaline, and I felt so out of control of my own mind and body. I was angrier than I had ever been before. I felt such rage, pure fury. And I knew in that second that I was done.

I was done with him. I was done with this life. I was done cowering. I was done being belittled. I was done being humiliated. I was done being silent. I was so far past done, and I knew before I even headed to find him and before any words left my mouth, that it was over. I was out. By any means necessary. I wasn't doing this for one more day.

God, that's it. I've had it. I'm done. Do what you will with me. Kill me if you have to, to get my mom and brother away from this madman, but I am not doing this for even one more day. My own dad just called me a slut. I can't bear it. I can't. I won't.

I felt my body charging down the hall, and I could hear my mom talking to me, but I couldn't make out anything more than my name. It was foggy; I couldn't see perfectly or hear perfectly. I felt like heat was leaving every pore in my body.

"What did you call me?" I yelled at him when I got less than five feet from my dad.

"You—" he started.

I didn't even let him finish. "I said what the hell did you just call me? A slut? Seriously? A slut! I have never even touched a boy. Never kissed a boy!"

"Don't you give me that bullshit! I saw you and your friend coming in from outside after the movie!"

"Yeah! Because we were looking for you! Here, I'll call the movie theater right now and you can ask the manager. He knows we were there. He saw us leaving at the end, and he said good-bye to us. I'll call him and prove you're wrong!"

"You're so full of shit, Jena! You were out there with some boy doing God knows what! You don't fool me. You may fool your mom, but you don't fool me!"

While he spewed his craziness, I called the theater. As it rang, I realized how stupid I was about to sound to the manager, but I had to push that thought to the back of my mind because this was really important.

"Hello. Regal Movies, how can I help you?"

"Hi, is this the manager?"

"Yes it is. How can I help you?"

"I was just there with my friend. We were the ones that got there late, and you said we could stay over and catch the beginning of the movie if we wanted, remember?"

"Sure, yes, I remember. Did you leave something here?"

"No, I just wanted you to tell my dad that we were there for the movie the whole time. He thinks we left, but you know we were there. You said good-bye to us at the end when we were leaving."

"Ummm, well yes, okay. I mean, yes I know you were here. I will tell him if you like," he said in a tone that made it abundantly clear how uncomfortable he was with the request.

"Here! Take the phone, Dad! It's the manager and he will tell you we were there the whole time!" I shoved the phone toward my dad as hard as I could.

"I'm not talking to him. I know what I saw, Jena!"

My mom took the phone from me as I continued yelling at my dad, "You won't take the phone because you know I'm right and you know you're the one that's full of shit!"

My dad slapped me across the face with such force that I fell back onto the kitchen table and knocked it over. As I rolled back over the top of the table, my head banged up against the wall. Enraged, I was on my feet before I could take my next breath. The only thing standing in between us now was the kitchen table that was flipped on its side.

"Yeah, that's right! Go ahead, Dad! That's what you always do! It's all you do! Hit women and children, right? You know what you are, Dad? You're a coward! And that's all you are!"

My dad's eyes turned black, and he closed the gap between us in a millisecond as he tossed the kitchen table out of the way like it was nothing. The next thing I felt was his fists on my face, and I fell to the floor. He pinned me up against the wall with the weight of his body as he leaned on me and continued to hit me furiously. I remember my face feeling wet. I remember peeing myself. I remember seeing my mom on his back trying to pull him off of me. I don't remember the pain. I remember telling God that I was ready to come home.

I can't tell you how long my dad pummeled my body before he

stopped. Of sheer exhaustion, I think. But when he finally did, he just plopped down in the closest kitchen chair and stared at me. Stared through me. With such hatred. Not remorse. Not disbelief at what he'd just done. No. It was hatred staring back at me. I didn't know what to do or how to feel. I hadn't planned on making it out of that alive. Only a minute or two passed, but it seemed like an eternity that I sat there trying to decide what to do next. My dad in the chair, my mom a few feet behind him crying, and me on the floor a mess. And then I saw it. The phone on the wall behind him. That ugly yellow rotary phone resting on the equally ugly flowered wallpaper.

God, I can't do this anymore. And I know that you know it. Please either protect me as I go for the phone or let him kill me quickly and get Mom and Nate out of this for good. But either way, God, I am done living this way.

I didn't know if I would be able to stand, but God didn't let my legs fail me. As I got to my feet, the urine that had puddled up underneath me ran down my jeans, and I took four steps and reached for the phone on the wall behind my dad. Seemed like it took forever for the 9 to roll back around into place before I could dial 1 and 1, but the phone quickly rang.

"911, what's your emergency?"

The sobs were instant, but I was able to get out, "My dad just beat me up, and I need someone to help me." And then I lost it, weeping out loud uncontrollably. I could hear the lady trying to talk to me, but I just couldn't stop crying.

I heard my dad's chair squeal across the floor as he whipped it around, realizing what I'd just done, and he jumped to his feet as he simultaneously ripped the phone from the wall.

As it came crashing to the kitchen floor, he glared at me and said, "You better take a good look around you and think long and hard before you do something you'll regret! I can promise you that you will NEVER live like this again!"

Finally. We *finally* agreed on something. It wasn't what he meant, I knew. It was hard to even make any sense of what he meant. How could he think that material things mattered to me when I'd never felt safe a day in my life. Never been unafraid for as long as I could remember. And he thought I should consider what house I lived in or what hung on the walls? I couldn't process it. What he was saying. I couldn't process any of it. But there it was in the end, wasn't it? I had finally faced my greatest fear head on and had stood up to my abuser, silenced no more. Willing to accept any consequence but one—that everything would stay the same.

Like all cowards who've been called out, my dad made a run for it before the red-and-blue lights and the sirens arrived. But it didn't matter; it was over. This was the beginning of the end of his reign of terror over us. As I rode in the back of the ambulance to the hospital with the EMTs and lady police officer assuring me that I was going to be okay and that I was safe now, I somehow drifted off to sleep. I think it was years of accumulated exhaustion meeting a moment where I truly felt safe and my body just gave out.

When I woke in the hospital to the frenzied sounds of beeps and ringing and buzzes, I saw my mom sitting in the chair next to me, sleeping, and it made me smile. We made it, I thought. We really made it out alive. That's the last thing I can remember thinking before drifting back into a deep sleep.

In the weeks and months to follow, there would be meetings with lawyers and court dates. I would be asked many questions by many people. I would testify in court against my father. And in the end, I would be asked a very important question. One I was more prepared to answer than I would have thought.

The judge asked to speak to me alone, and when the lawyer and my mom told me, I was pretty nervous. The whole court thing made me pretty nervous, as I'd never told anyone about the things that had happened to us, and now all of these people were asking about it and in such an official setting. But I agreed to talk to him.

I pushed open the heavy wooden door to his office and saw an older gray-haired man motioning me to come in.

"Hello, young lady. Come on in, please. Have a seat," he said. "I wanted to talk to you about what's going to happen tomorrow. And I have a very important question for you, Jena. Do you think you can help me?"

"I'll try," I said.

"Good, that's all I ask, Jena. I know this has all been very hard on you and your family. And I want to do what's best for you going forward. Do you understand?"

I nodded.

"But I can't be sure I'm doing that without asking you what you want to see happen. What do you want to happen with your dad?"

"I just want it to stop. I want Mom, Nate and me to be safe."

"Well, I can certainly understand that, Jena. And you are safe now, I promise you that. And so are your mom and brother. Okay?

But what I'm asking you is what do you think should happen to your dad?"

I wasn't sure why he was asking me, but it felt good that he cared what I thought. I wasn't used to anyone asking me what I thought about anything.

"I don't know. I mean, I know that I don't want to have to ever see my dad again unless I want to. And I don't want him to come near my mom again. But I don't want him to go to jail if that's what you mean. My dad is already in jail, and I think he probably always will be. If there was some way you could get help for my dad, then I would like that. If you could help him to get better. But I still don't want to have to see him. I guess that's what I would want," I said, wondering if what I'd just said was okay.

"Thank you, Jena. The first thing I can tell you is that you won't have to see your dad unless you choose to on your own accord, okay? So I don't want you worrying about that. And I'm proud of you for wanting to see your dad get the help he needs. He does need help, Jena. You probably know that far better than me. So we'll see what we can do about that too, okay? One more question for you and then you can go. Do you want to be in the courtroom tomorrow for my decision? You don't have to be—it's up to you."

"No thanks. I really don't want to have to go back in there."

"That's all I needed to know. Thanks for being willing to talk to me, young lady. Why don't you head back out in the hall and find your mom now, okay?"

Before I could get to the door he said, "Jena, I want you to know that you're going to be okay. And your mom and your brother too.

It's going to take time. There's a lot of healing to do. But the life that's waiting for you can be anything you want it to be. You have to believe that. Just don't give up. Don't ever give up. Okay?"

Holding back the tears, I smiled and said, "I won't give up."

And I didn't, and I haven't.

As I swung open the heavy door, I could see my mom sitting in the hallway. She jumped to her feet and ran over and hugged me.

"Are you okay, Jena?"

"Yes, Mom. I'm good. Can we go home now?"

"Yes, let's go home. Are you hungry? I can take you to McDonald's if you want?"

"Can we just get it to go, Mom? I want to go home."

"Sure, honey, let's do that."

"The judge said I don't have to come tomorrow. Today is my last day. I'm so glad."

"That's great. I'm so glad too."

"I just want to eat and go home and take a nap. Is that okay?"

"Of course. That sounds like a good plan to me."

Our new home was a very small, run-down rental house on the far side of town, as far away from our old house as you could get and still be in the same town. My dad stayed in the home we grew up in.

My mom would later tell me that the judge gave my dad a suspended jail sentence with the stipulation that he would have to attend anger management and alcohol abuse classes and counseling. The judge ordered that I didn't have to have any contact or visitation with my dad unless I decided to on my own sometime in the future.

He left it up to my brother as to whether or not he wanted to see my dad. And my dad had to stay away from my mom indefinitely. We never really discussed it again at any length. And because there was no court in our town, we'd had to travel an hour for the court proceedings, so my dad's secrets were still safe from everyone he knew and from everyone that knew us. I think I was okay with that at the time because my load was plenty heavy without having to figure out a way to explain our lives to everyone else. But I did hear Nate tell his friend Steve that my dad had moved his girlfriend into the house. All I could think when I heard that was, he's all yours, lady.

Chapter 12

The Last Race

After a few weeks, I was finally back at school with everyone wondering why I had been out for so long. I told them I'd been out of town with my mom, dealing with family stuff. I don't think anyone bought it, but they let it slide. It felt strange being back in this place that I had dreaded for so long, it felt different. I still wasn't excited to be there, but it didn't feel as burdensome as it usually had.

And I knew I still had something really important I had to deal with. Track. For the first time in my life, I was in a position to call my own shots, and I knew with absolute certainty that track and field held no place in my future. But I wasn't sure how to handle it. I didn't want to just walk out on the team, but I was no longer willing to suffer through another season. I decided to go to practice after school and play it by ear. About halfway through, practice I realized what I wanted to do, what I felt I needed to do. But I kept it to myself. I'd wait for the big invitational meet the next night and do something I hadn't been able to do once in all my years of track.

That night at home, I asked my mom over dinner if she would

mind not coming to my meet the following night. She reluctantly agreed, but I knew she was wondering what was going on. She didn't press me on it, but she did ask me how I would get home. I told her I'd catch a ride with Kelsey. Our new house was less than a mile from the school.

It was nice sitting at the dinner table with Nate and Mom, just the three of us. I liked it. A lot. And though our dinner table was actually a fold-out card table and our chairs were plastic chairs we would typically use on the porch, I didn't care in the least. My dad was right; we never did live lavishly again. Gone were the nice cars and houses. Gone were the nice furnishings and brand-name clothes. My dad did everything imaginable to my mom to make her pay for leaving him, including withholding his child support. And my mom refused alimony, though she definitely needed it. Before marrying my dad, she'd had a good job working in Washington, DC. But after they were married, he hadn't allowed her to work outside the home, and he never let her have any money of her own. Everything was his. So when we left, the only job my mom could find right away was at a Hardees fast-food restaurant. And there were many nights the only food we had to eat was the leftover food she was allowed to bring home after her shift.

And though I heard my mom cry herself to sleep often, worrying how she would be able to take care of us and make ends meet, I didn't mind our new circumstances at all. And Nate didn't either. He and I both started working after school, me at the golf course washing golf carts and Nate at the local drive-thru. We worked hard, and we worked together, and we made it just fine. We had everything that actually mattered. We had something that money could never buy—love. And stability.

I cleaned up the kitchen for Mom after dinner so she could go sit on the porch and relax. As I wiped down the card table, I thought about my upcoming track meet. I was completely satisfied with the decision I had made.

When I woke the next morning, I could smell bacon cooking in the kitchen, and I couldn't wait to have a slice. I wasn't able to eat every morning yet, but there were some mornings that I would wake with an appetite, and I could tell it made my mom really happy when I'd sit down and eat breakfast with her and Nate. This morning it was French toast and bacon, and it really hit the spot. After breakfast, I got ready for school and packed my track uniform in my bag along with my spikes. I hugged my mom good-bye and knew I wouldn't see her until later that night. She had a long shift at Hardee's that day, and it would have been tough for her to make it to my meet anyway. Besides, this was something I really needed to do alone.

As I arrived at school, I heard Kelsey yell, "Jena!" I could hear her before I could see her through the crowd of students racing every which way through the halls that morning. "Hey, girl! You ready for tonight?" she said as she held her hand up to high-five me.

I laughed out loud and shook my head. "Yeah, you know, I'm just so excited for tonight. When am I not just so thrilled to attend a track meet?" I rolled my eyes.

"Oh, come on now. You know it's gonna be the bomb, and you know you're gonna be the bomb. It's all in the way you look at it, Jena. I keep telling you that, but you don't listen!" She smiled.

"Yeah, yeah. I know. *That's* the problem, I never listen." I smiled back.

"All right, see you later, okay?" she said before heading to class.

"Later, Kelsey." I couldn't help but laugh again.

Classes seemed to go by quicker than usual, and before I knew it, the bell was ringing and it was time to start thinking about what I needed to do in a few hours. No one was going to understand. And no one was going to like it. But I'd accepted that, deciding that for this one night, this one meet, I needed to please only myself.

While most of the girls and boys on the track team walked down to the local sub shop to eat and kill some time before all the other teams started to arrive, I ducked out back and headed to the track. This would be the first time I'd ever voluntarily gone out on a track without it being a mandatory practice or meet. Normally the track was the last place on earth I'd ever want to be. But I needed to make peace with this heap of asphalt, and I needed to take back the power I'd given it over me all these years. As I entered through the gates, it looked like a ghost town. Not a soul was out there. I made my way around to the starting line of the 400 meters. To be exact, I made my way around to the starting line of lane 4 of the 400 meters. Lane 4 and I were well acquainted with one another. Lane 4 is the lane where the person with the fastest time in the heat is placed. Lane 4 and I had a very long, very strained history. But I was determined that lane 4 was no longer going to rule me. I sat there saying good-bye to the sport I'd hated for so long and with such passion. And I thought for the first time how sad it was that I was never able to enjoy the only God-given talent I had. I didn't think it was supposed to be that way.

I sat there so long my legs stuck to the track when I went to get up. I laughed and thought to myself that the track was trying to hang onto me for just a little while longer. "No way," I said, "you and I are through for good!" I looked around to see if anyone could see me talking to the track. That notion made me laugh even harder.

I made it back through the gates just in time to see the first bus pull in. This meet was a big deal. Normally we wouldn't even be invited. But because I and one other girl who was a long distance runner had made such a name for ourselves throughout the region, our team had been invited and our school had been asked to host the meet. We definitely had the best track in the entire district, no question about that. Ours put most of the other schools' tracks to shame. My coach had found me in the hall twice that day to remind me that there would be people there that evening that were coming just to see me run. To see what I could do. If it were any other day, any other meet prior, I'd have spent the day throwing up in the bathroom, but I wasn't scared of this meet. I wasn't nervous at all. I knew what I wanted to do, and I was trying to just stay focused on that.

Before I knew it, the infield lights were on, the announcer was speaking, and the meet had begun. For the first time ever, my coach decided not to put me in any field events so I could just focus on running. It made me wonder if it was because he took so much heat from other coaches in our district for spreading me too thin. I had heard other coaches chastise him for that all the time. I guess it didn't really matter to me why he chose not to put me in the field events. I was glad. That meant my very first event would be the 200 meters. I was scheduled to run the 200, 400, and the last leg of the mile relay, which was another 400. I sat through the field events and enjoyed cheering my teammates on. I was always mesmerized by the high jumpers, especially the guys. They could just fly through the air. It was mind blowing how they could jump over a bar that was taller than they were.

Finally, it was time for the running events, and the stands were packed. Usually track and field didn't have that many spectators, but our track team usually had more spectators than most schools. Anytime we had a standout athlete in our school, the stands were packed all season. Laura won the 100 meters, with her sister taking second place. I knew they were glad I wasn't in that race but not half as glad as I was.

Then I heard, "First call to the infield for the 200 meters. First call to the infield for the 200 meters." *Here we go. It's time. I can't mess this up.* There are four heats, so I have to wait for the last heat. No one else from my team is in the last heat for the 200 but me. If this were a district race, Laura would probably have been in this heat with me, but since there were so many schools here, she and her sister were in the earlier heats. I was glad about that too. I didn't like going head to head with either of them. They didn't much like it either. Though, if they knew what I had planned, they wouldn't mind tonight.

Finally, it was time for my heat to run. We found our lanes on the track and adjusted our starting blocks. After a few minutes, the announcer began his introductions. I tuned him out as best I could, trying to stay calm, but the crowd roared when he said, "In lane 4, number 11, Jena Parks!" I knew I should wave to acknowledge their kind reception, but I just couldn't, not considering what I was about to do. The announcer said, "Runners take your mark... set..." The gun fired and then quickly fired again. There was a false start. And a momentary pause before the announcer said, "Lane 4 is disqualified for false starting, please remove your blocks from the track." I heard a flood of gasps from the stands and then total silence as I picked up my blocks and moved off the track.

I was so glad that Coach White was all the way down at the finish line because I knew he was furious. And I was hoping to avoid him at all costs. As soon as the race started, I made my way down the sideline and out the front gate of the track. I slipped into the locker room and into one of the bathroom stalls, locked the door, and just sat there. I let out a huge sigh and felt both relief as well as a tinge of anxiety. I had false started before on purpose, but not at such an important meet. Important to my coach. And to my school. Not important to me. But still, important. And suddenly I felt guilty, like I had just let a lot of people down. But I pushed that feeling down and reminded myself that I got to have one meet where I let it be about me, just this one time. I'd more than paid my dues. I deserved this one night. I kept telling myself this over and over, thinking if I said it enough, I'd believe it.

I could hear some girls in the locker room now, and I could tell from the voices that it was the twins from my team. "Oh, please! You know she did that on purpose! She can't handle the pressure. She never could!" I heard Laura say.

"I don't care why it happened, I'm just glad we don't have to hear, 200 meters, first place, Jena Parks, on the morning announcements!" Jessica said, and they both laughed out loud.

I pulled my feet up to the toilet seat, hoping they didn't realize I was in there. I plugged my ears because I didn't want to hear them say anything else mean about me. They had no idea what I'd been through or how hard it was for me to even be there. But I resolved not to let them steal this night from me. This was my night. The one track meet where I was in control of what happened.

Several minutes went by, and I took my fingers out of my ears. The coast was clear, but I stayed in there until I heard last call for the 400 meters. I was sure my coach was going nuts trying to find me so he could ask me what happened in the 200. I raced into the infield just in time to take my spot on the track, lane 4 of the 400 meters. I looked down at my starting blocks, and I felt like I might start crying, so I looked up at the sky. *No Jena, no, not here, not now. No, you are not going to cry. You're going to see this through to the end. You're going to do it your way. Focus.*

Out of the corner of my eye, I saw my coach, and I could feel him staring at me, but I didn't dare look his way. I couldn't take a chance on messing this up.

As the introductions were made, the crowd cheered loudly as he announced my lane assignment. Everyone knew this was my race, and they were expecting big things from me tonight.

"Runners on your mark...set..." Gunfire. Gunfire. I kept looking straight down at the track as I paced back and forth with my hands on my hips, just waiting to hear the announcer's voice.

"Lane 4 is disqualified for false starting. Please remove your blocks from the track."

I took my blocks and headed off the outside of the track, not the inside where my coach was standing with the other coaches. I didn't dare look their way. I knew everyone was floored because they expected to see the best 400 meter sprinter in the region win that race tonight and instead she was walking off the track, blocks in hand, disqualified.

I had the same plan as before to head to the locker room and wait for the relay, but this time I was stopped before I could even get to the gate by three of my teammates.

"What in the hell was that, Jena? What are you doing? You know these people are here to see you run and you couldn't care less! What is wrong with you? You don't think about anyone but yourself, do you? You act like a spoiled brat, Jena, really! Get over yourself!"

I couldn't even believe what Megan had just said to me. None of it was true. None of it described me! But I had too much going on in my own head to deal with her right now. And if I opened my mouth, I'd just start crying and say a bunch of things I didn't really mean. So I walked right through them and kept going until I got into the locker room. This time I was smart enough to head through the locker room and into the gym. It was dark in there, and no one would look for me there.

One more race Jena, one more. The only race you care about is next. Focus on that, I keep telling myself. Once I'd regained my composure, I headed back through the locker room and out onto the track. The mile relay was right after the four hundred, and I was ready. I was ready to run. I was ready to run just one race for me, because I chose to. Not because I had to or because everyone expected me to. This one race was for me. And I didn't feel any pressure at all. This was a team race. It wasn't about me. It was about us. And I never let my teammates down when I'm part of the relay race.

"Jena! Jena!" I heard my coach yelling as I made my way to the infield. "What in the hell have you done here tonight? You've let everyone down. Me, your teammates, yourself! I can't believe you did this on a night as big as this one. Do you have any idea how many kids would give anything to be in your shoes tonight? How many kids would love to have schools like Clemson and Columbia interested in them? Do you?"

"Maybe all of them would, Coach, I don't know! But not me. Not me! I just want to run this relay race and go home!"

"You're not going anywhere near that relay race, Jena! You think I'd let you jeopardize the team for the sake of your immature display of what? I don't even know what to call it! But you're not running the relay. You may as well head in the locker room, change, and head home. You're done for the night!"

"Coach White! I need to run the relay race! I want to run the relay race."

"Oh, you want to run the relay race? You want to run this race? But not that race or the other race? What do you think this is, Jena? You're a part of a team, and the team relies on you to lead, to win.

And you failed them tonight. I'm not going to take a chance on you ruining their chances of a win in the relay. Hell, I don't even know what I'm saying. We can't win without you. I'll give you that. But I'd rather lose with a team that gives me everything than put you on that track again tonight! Go home!"

As Coach White stormed off into the infield, my heart sank. This couldn't be happening. This wasn't part of the plan. The plan was I would finally get to run one race that I actually wanted to run, one race where it wasn't about me and the pressure wasn't on me. Just one race, by choice, not because someone else was making me run, but because I wanted to. How could he take this from me after all the races I'd won for him over the years? After all the tears and throwing up and agony, and he couldn't let me have just one race. No way. No way. I wouldn't accept that.

I ran into the infield where my relay teammates were lining up, and I could see that he'd put Hannah in my place to run the last leg. Hannah hated the 400 and was mediocre at it at best. Why would he put her there?

"Hannah…Hannah…let me take your place. Okay?"

She looked confused and said, "Jena, I can't just let you take my place. Coach would be furious with me. He's already angry enough with you. No. You're not taking my place."

"But, Hannah, you hate this race. You know you do. And you're going to have to run the last leg in the fastest heat. Don't do it. Just let me step on the track in your place. I'll take the blame for it. I'll just jump in place at the last second. Please. Hannah, look, I know we don't get along, but you know what I've done for this team, please, just give me this one race. I won't screw it up, I promise. Please?"

Cara, who was running the lead off leg, piped up, "Jena, she said no! Just leave it alone!" and with that she headed onto the track.

"Runners on your mark...set...go!" and they were off. By the time they hit the last corner, Cara was in fourth place of eight. She handed off to Lisa, and by the time they hit the last turn, we were in sixth place. As Kelly stepped into place for the third leg, I could see Hannah's face drop. She didn't want to run the last leg and I knew it. Heck, at this point I was wondering if I even wanted to run it. We were so far behind. But I quickly reminded myself it wasn't about winning tonight, not in the sense of crossing the line first. For me it was just about wanting to run, wanting to see what I could do when I wasn't scared to death, when I wasn't under pressure. I didn't know because I'd never ever been in that position. But this was my chance. My last chance.

Before Kelly even got to the first turn, Hannah looked at me and said, "Okay, Jena, you take it. But you tell Coach that you made that decision, not me. Just make it look like you jumped out there to take it, okay?"

"Okay." I smiled at her. "Hannah...thanks...really...thanks."

"I don't know why you're thanking me. Look, we are in last place by at least 20 meters. Better your loss than mine."

Coach patted Hannah on the back and said, "Just do your best, even Parks couldn't pull this one out."

Hannah was startled because she hadn't seen him there, but I had seen him coming. I just shook my head at Hannah as if to tell her not to say anything. As they entered the third corner of the track, we were so far behind it was hopeless, but I didn't care. It wasn't the scenario I had been hoping for, but maybe it was the one I needed. No pressure to win. Just running to see what my best really was.

I jumped out onto the track into position to take the hand off, and I heard Coach White say, "What the hell…"

Next thing I knew the baton was in my hand and I was off. I'd never seen people in front of me in a 400 before, and so far in front of me at that, but I was undaunted. I pumped my arms like mad, and by the time we hit the second corner, I'd cut their lead in half. I didn't know how I'd done it, but I felt unstoppable. I could hear the crowd yelling loudly, "Go, Jena, go! Go, Jena, you can do it!" My heart was pounding out of my chest, but my body was all machine, clicking on all cylinders, and by the third turn, I was within striking distance of the rest of the field. I had never been so determined in my life. And when we reached the final straightaway, I had pulled ahead of half of the field and was closing in on the rest.

I could hear my coach's voice above all others now, and I could see from the corner of my eye that he was running down the track with me, inside the infield. "Jena, go, pump your arms, go, you can do it! Jena, push! Push, Jena! You can do it!"

With the finish line in sight, I was tied with the girl in the third lane. I pumped harder, harder, and I leaned, and I did it! We won! We won the relay! We did it! I couldn't breathe, and I couldn't stand up. But as I fell on the grass in the infield, I was so happy. Beyond happy. I felt ecstatic! My coach fell to the ground beside me and said, "Look, Jena, look!" He showed me his stopwatch with my split time. "Three seconds, Jena! You shaved three seconds off of your best time! Unbelievable. You are unbelievable, kid! Way to go! Can you breathe?"

He got to his feet and pulled me to mine. He gave me a huge bear hug and said, "I wouldn't have thought that anyone, including you, could have pulled out a win in that race tonight. That was nothing short of miraculous, Jena. Way to go kid. Way to go!"

By now the rest of my teammates were wrapped around me, and we were all jumping up and down, so thrilled to have won! None of us knew how we'd managed it, but we had and that was all that mattered. That, and I had finally run a race because I wanted to. And it felt so good and so freeing. I congratulated my teammates and started to head off the track when Cara said, "Where are you going? We have a podium to stand on and a medal to receive!"

"You guys go, enjoy it. I'm good." I could tell they didn't understand, but the look on their faces let me know that they were good with it too. And with that, I left the track for the very last time, content and fully satisfied. I could finally file this chapter of my life away and move on to something else. Something of my choosing.

Right as I was about to step out of the gate, I heard Kelsey say, "Mmmmm hmmmm. You thought you were gonna dodge me all night, didn't you? You know you did." She smiled and hugged me. "Girl, I have never seen anyone run so fast in all my life. That was amazing! And you're smiling too, what is that about? Nah, don't answer me, I don't even need to know. It's just good to see you smiling while standing on the track!"

"Well, technically I'm off the track," I said, smiling back at her.

"Oh yeah? Smiling and you got jokes too, huh? Okay. Okay.

Cute." She laughed. "You need a ride?"

"Thanks, Kelsey but I'm gonna walk. But, hey, do you want to come over tomorrow and play some basketball?"

She looked so surprised; I'd never asked her to come to my house before. "Sure! Yeah! What time?"

"Noon?"

"I'll be there. You be safe, yeah? You know these folks around here can't drive!"

"I will. See you tomorrow."

I jogged home, and by the time I got there, my mom had made a pizza for us so we could watch a movie together. You know those pizzas you make from a kit in a box? That was the only pizza we could afford, but it was fine by me. It was a perfect way to end the night. My mom didn't ask me what had happened on the track until the next day. We curled up on the couch with our pizza, watching movies, and were just happy to be together.

I slept so well that night, better than I could ever remember sleeping, and when my alarm went off, I remembered that Kelsey was coming over. I jumped out of bed to find my mom because I'd forgotten to ask her if it was okay the night before. Turned out it was more than okay; I think she was more excited that I was having a friend over than I was.

"That's great, Jena! I'll make you girls some lunch later on. Good for you!" She beamed.

"I'm going to go change, Mom. Let me know when Kelsey gets here."

"I will."

By the time I got back to the kitchen, Kelsey was standing there with one of the cinnamon rolls my mom had made for breakfast in her mouth. I couldn't help but laugh. Kelsey could never pass up good food. I didn't know how she stayed so skinny eating like she did.

"Hey, Jen Jen!" she said between bites.

"Hey, Kelsey, you ready to play some basketball?"

"You know I am, let's go!" She stuffed the rest of the roll in her mouth and grabbed the ball out of my hands.

As we headed out to the court behind our house, I thought about what a gorgeous day it was. The sun was shining but it wasn't too hot. There was a slight breeze. And I felt good. I felt really good. Happy.

Kelsey and I loved to play horse even though I'd never beaten her once. We were on our third game when I saw Kelsey's eyes get as big as saucers.

"Oh my gosh, girl, don't look now, but coming up your driveway is that hopeless fool Jason! I swear! I'm not kidding you. You gotta give him credit, he's determined, that's for sure! Oh my goodness gracious, Jena. This boy has got it some kinda bad! Wow. If at first you don't succeed, try, try again, right? Hahaha, no seriously, I hear he's really nice. You should at least hear him out. I mean, look, he's coming with some candy, a flower, a Slurpeeeeeeee! You know that's your favorite. Wait, how does he know that? Has he been stalking you? Haha, you know I'm messing with you. He's just done his homework, that's all! Don't be nervous. Girl, you have to at least let him say his piece. After all the effort he's put in. Lord have mercy! I don't even know what to think. He's either the best thing since sliced bread or he's obsessed! Hahaha."

I beamed the ball at Kelsey for taunting me. "Kelsey! Don't even kid around about that!"

"Girl, you know I'm playing with you. Jason is as harmless as they come. He's just a big ole,' strapping, laid-back country boy with a crazy crush on you! Awww, he's going to be on this court in about ten seconds. Just say hi, that's all you gotta do, Jena. I'm sure he'll take it from there."

I turned around and saw Jason standing there with chocolate-covered peanuts, a cola Slurpee—both my favorites—and a single red rose. I was embarrassed but moved by Jason's thoughtfulness. "Hi…Are those for me? You have all my favorites. How did you know?" I smiled.

Jason handed the gifts to me as his face turned every possible shade of red. "I see you in 7-11 sometimes, and I was pretty sure this is what I've seen you buy. I hope you like them."

"I do, thank you. That was really nice of you. This is Kelsey."

"Hey, Kelsey," Jason said, extending his hand.

"You don't need to be all that formal now…but I will take some of those chocolates off Jena's hands right there." Kelsey high-fived Jason while reaching for the chocolate-covered peanuts.

"We were just shooting around. Do you want to play?" I offered.

"Sure, yeah, I'd love to."

And for that one brief snapshot in time, I wasn't thinking about everything that had come before, and I certainly couldn't know the struggles that lay ahead. In that moment I was just a regular teenage girl like any other, enjoying hanging out with my best friend playing basketball in the warm summer breeze and exploring a new crush. It was the first time I could remember being fully present, where I wasn't thinking ten steps ahead. No fear. No anxiety. Just joy. And peace. Finally, peace. And as I walked over to the edge of the court to find a place to set Jason's gifts down, I felt the tears well up once more, but these were altogether different than any tears I'd ever felt before. They weren't borne of pain or fear. No. They were happy tears. I smiled and thought, *Thank you, God. Thank you.*

Thank You

Thank you for taking the time to read *The Fear of the Blow*. If you enjoyed it, please consider telling your friends and posting a short review on Amazon.com. Word-of-mouth referrals are an author's best friend and greatly appreciated.

About the Author

Jena Parks. Champion of the underdog. Survivor of domestic violence. Seeker of peace. Lover of simplicity. Anchored in faith. And grateful for everyday blessings. Jena Parks' lifelong journey to find refuge from the constant fear and intense anxiety that has plagued her since early childhood led her to author the autobiographical series, *The Fear of the Blow*. Based on Jena's real-life experiences with domestic violence and alcoholism, the series chronicles her journey from youth to adulthood and her quest to find lasting peace and happiness.

Jena's first release, *The Fear of the Blow: A Young Woman's Gut-Wrenching Story of Child Abuse, Domestic Violence, Alcoholism, and Redemption* is available now. In it you'll discover a young girl's unrelenting will and determination to ensure the very survival of her family from the extreme brutality and cruelty of her father. As the second installment unfolds, *The Fear of the Blow: The Discovery Years*, Jena has become a fiercely independent young woman determined to leave her troubled past in her rearview mirror and forge her own path. Follow her to Venezuela, deep in the heart of the Amazon jungle, where at the age of eighteen she lives in a Yanomamo Indian village with an American missionary family for eight adventure-packed weeks. Then take a front row seat as she discovers a forbidden first love on the Orient Express with a mysterious man who'll open up her world and heart in ways she never dreamed possible. As Jena travels from London to Paris, Switzerland to Italy, she knows she's still just running…running from the truth, one that she's going to have to face sooner or later. Be there to find out how Jena's estranged relationship with her father comes to a tragic end.

Email: itsjenaparks@gmail.com
Twitter: @itsjenaparks